a busy woman's guide to prayer

a busy woman's guide to prayer

forget the guilt and find the gift

cheri fuller

INTEGRITY®

PUBLISHERS

Nashville

A BUSY WOMAN'S GUIDE TO PRAYER

Published by Integrity Publishers, a division of Integrity Media, Inc., 5250 Virginia Way, Suite 110, Brentwood, TN 37027.

HELPING PEOPLE WORLDWIDE EXPERIENCE *the* MANIFEST PRESENCE *of* GOD.

Published in association with the literary agency of Alive Communications, Inc., 7680 Goddard Street, Suite 200, Colorado Springs, Colorado 80920.

Unless otherwise indicated, all Scripture quotations are taken from The Holy Bible, New Living Translation® (NLT®). Copyright © 1996. Used by permission of Tyndale House Publishers, Inc., Wheaton, Illinois 60189. All rights reserved.

Other Scripture quotations are taken from the following sources: The Amplified Bible (AMP), New Testament. Copyright © 1954, 1958, 1962, 1964, 1965, 1987 by The Lockman Foundation. Used by permission. All rights reserved. The Amplified Bible (AMP), Old Testament. Copyright © 1965, 1987 by the Zondervan Corporation. Used by permission. All rights reserved. The Message (MSG) by Eugene H. Peterson. Copyright © 1993, 1994, 1995, 1996, 2000, 2001, 2002. Used by permission of NavPress Publishing Group. All rights reserved. The New American Standard Bible® (NASB®). Copyright © 1960, 1062, 1963, 1968, 1971, 1972, 1973, 1975, 1977, 1995 by The Lockman Foundation. Used by permission. The Authorized King James Version of the Bible (KJV). The Holy Bible, New International Version® (NIV®). Copyright © 1973, 1978, 1984 by International Bible Society. Used by permission of Zondervan. All rights reserved. The Living Bible (TLB). Copyright © 1971 by Tyndale House Publishers, Inc. Used by permission. All rights reserved. The New King James Version® (NKJV®). Copyright © 1982 by Thomas Nelson, Inc. Used by permission. All rights reserved.

Cover Design: Brand Navigation, LLC—DeAnna Pierce, Bill Chiaravalle,
                    www. brandnavigation.com
Author Cover Photograph: David Fitzgerald
Cover Image: Stephen Gardner, Pixelworks Studio
Interior Design: Inside Out Design & Typesetting

Names and details in some of the author's anecdotes and illustrations may have been changed to protect the subjects' privacy.

The title of this book was inspired by the author's article, "A Busy Woman's Guide to Prayer—No Matter How Packed Your Daily Planner Is!" in *Today's Christian Woman,* March/April 2004, and a portion of chapter 11, "Praying for Your Enemies," first appeared as "Who, Me? Pray for *Her?*" in the magazine's November/December 2001 issue.

Library of Congress Cataloging-in-Publication Data

Fuller Cheri.
    A busy woman's guide to prayer / by Cheri Fuller.
       p. cm.
    Summary: "Readers will experience the power of having a vibrant life of prayer, a relationship with God, and discover creative ideas to weave prayer into the fabric of their day"—Provided by publisher.

ISBN 1-59145-321-6 (tradepaper)

1. Christian women—Religious life.   2. Prayer—Christianity.   I. Title.
BV4527.F843   2005
248.3'2'082—dc22   20050173458

Printed in the United States of America
05 06 07 08 DPS 9 8 7 6 5 4 3 2 1

Dedicated to our beloved "Mimi," Joan Fuller.
Though she stays busy caring for others
in her community of Pawhuska, Oklahoma,
she's a faithful, praying woman—
and the most fun grandma and mother I know.
You have blessed us all!

Contents

contents

Acknowledgments

Ĭ am especially grateful to Holmes, my praying-without-ceasing husband, for his support, prayers, and love not only as I wrote this book but in our thirty-five years of marriage together. I love you.

To our sons and daughter and their spouses: Justin and Tiff, Chris and Maggie, Ali and Hans, and to our five grandchildren: Caitlin, Caleb, Noah, Josephine, and Luke, thank you for *your* prayers for us. You light up our lives, and it gives us much joy to pray for you and see your lives unfold!

I am so grateful for the intercessors, that cloud of witnesses who surround us and have graced us with their wisdom through the ages. From them I have gained much insight for my own prayer life and for this book, especially Flo Perkins, Andrew Murray, O. Hallesby, E. M. Bounds, Oswald Chambers, Derek Prince, Corrie ten Boom, Catherine Marshall, Amy Carmichael, Henri Nouwen, and others.

Heartfelt thanks to my prayer partners who have prayed for the

acknowledgments

writing of this book and for our family with such love and faithfulness: Patty Johnson, Peggy and Earl Stewart, Jo Hayes, Janet Page, Mimi, Lynn, Dru Fuller, Betsy West, Anne Denmark, Melanie Hemry, Brenda Steen; and to fellow moms in our community's military support group: Ruthie Gardosik, Cecilia Martin, Lucy Trotman, and Jeanne Fell. I appreciate you more than you could know.

Thanks to Joey Paul and Integrity Publishers for your belief in this message and your partnership with me. To Lee Hough, my literary agent, for your encouragement and representation.

And to all the women I've spoken to at retreats and conferences who have told me about the struggles and joys of their prayer lives; what you've shared has helped shape this book. To Speak Up, and to Carol and Gene Kent, dear friends who represent me so well in my ministry.

To each, please accept my heartfelt gratitude.

PART ONE

A Fresh Look at Prayer

1

A Mary Heart with a Martha Schedule

The one concern of the devil is to keep Christians from praying. . . .
The prayer of the feeblest saint on earth who keeps right with God
paralyzes the darkness—that's why he tries to keep our minds fussy
in active work until we cannot think in prayer.

—Oswald Chambers

LIKE MARTHA IN THE BIBLE, I have lots to do—office work, writing projects, laundry, cooking, cleaning. The week I was beginning this book, for instance, I had a deadline to meet, but my daughter-in-law was hospitalized, and I gladly stepped in to care for her toddler. Add in meals to cook, a household to run, a prayer group to lead, and preparation for a ministry trip. Is it any wonder I felt rushed?

Doctors call the newest disorder of the twenty-first century the "hurry-up sickness," and lots of us have it. Our lives are driven by Day-Timers, to-do lists, and assorted demands, and we never seem to have enough time to get it all done.

Maybe, like me, you do a lot of multitasking, like when I was driving to an appointment across town recently and stopped at a red light. A quick look in the mirror as I glanced at the mass of traffic behind me told me I might scare someone at the meeting without some makeup. I'd had to race out of the house after two calls detained me, so I was in a rush to make it to the meeting anywhere close to on time. I got out my concealer and smoothed it under my weary eyes and then was digging for my lipstick when the cell phone rang.

"Mom, Noah and Luke both woke up sick and need medicine the doctor called in and also some Motrin. Hans has the car, and I'm stranded. Could you pick it up for me?"

"Sure, honey. I'll bring it by after the meeting," I answered, hurriedly jotting down a reminder on a sticky note before the light changed. When the cell phone rang again, it was my friend Peggy reminding me about our Bible study group that night. As I drove on down Broadway Extension, three more things popped into my mind that I needed to take care of in addition to picking up the medicine for my grandsons (and also some milk): I had a radio interview to do at 4:00, a column due for a Web site I write for, and the dog had to have his shots. Those tasks went on the sticky note too.

Just as you may have experienced, I've had seasons like this where I've found it a real challenge to squeeze in time for a deep breath, much less have quiet moments for prayer.

So do many women.

There's my friend Jennifer, whose day starts at 5:30 a.m. with a workout at the gym. Besides being a city attorney, she is the primary caregiver for both her parents and her mother-in-law, who suffers with Alzheimer's. She also chairs the building committee at her church and tries to meet with her girlfriend for an occasional lunch so she doesn't burn out completely.

Then there's BethAnn, a new friend I met recently from Spokane, Washington. She has five children, including *two sets of twins*. She works full time in the real estate business and is also a singer-songwriter who leads worship at her church and at women's retreats and conferences. This is one busy woman. Her biggest challenge is internal discipline and carving out a regular daily portion of quiet time. Everything in the outside world screams demands at her around the clock. Kids, husband, house, errands, ministry, business, and appointments constantly vie for her attention, and she struggles to discipline herself to be a human "being" instead of a human "doing" in the midst of all that.

Carey is a high school teacher from Ohio who is working on her master's degree at night. She and her husband are in their first year of marriage and, sort of like ships passing in the night, they feel like cars passing in the driveway. She'd love to spend more time with him. She'd also love to have more time with God, but when she finally settles down for quiet time, she's so tired she falls asleep.

Lauren has four active kids who are all involved in extracurricular activities, sports, and church programs. Besides coaching her daughters' basketball team, Lauren volunteers at her children's school and hosts a weekly sports radio program that she writes, produces, and

MCs. When Lauren described her life to me, I wondered, *When does she sleep?*

PRAY WITHOUT CEASING

The first time I read the verse in the Bible that tells us to "pray without ceasing" (1 Thessalonians 5:17 KJV), I thought, *Does Paul know about my schedule?* Surely Paul must have had an assistant—unlike most of us!

Pray without ceasing? Certainly Paul never juggled career and home responsibilities like we do today, never corralled a houseful of energetic kids 24/7. Even senior women bemoan their lack of time. "I thought I was going to have an easy schedule and more time on my hands after I was an empty-nester, but I'm busier than I've ever been," a Connecticut woman told me. Would you like to show Paul *your* Day-Timer and ask him exactly where he'd slot in this "pray without ceasing" activity?

There's not a woman out there who wants to be hurried, who wakes up in the morning hoping she'll have to frantically rush through the day to get everything done that her family or her job or her lifestyle requires of her. But the fact is, that's the reality for millions of women today; we are overwhelmingly busy. Everything's moving faster and faster in the world around us. A recent survey showed that 36 percent of Americans say they are constantly rushed, and women more than most. Many of us feel exhausted and over-loaded—even when we're exhausted by and overloaded with work, people, and activities we love and enjoy.

6

Single, working women lead some of the most hectic lives on the planet. Teachers I know get up at 5:00 a.m. and work until late at night, grading and planning for the next day's instruction. Many at-home moms not only nurture their kids but also homeschool them and/or run part-time home businesses to make ends meet. It's difficult to balance our lives and juggle the time demands of family and home, work, church, spiritual life—much less find moments for fun or renewal.

Most of us can identify with Dana, who stopped me at a recent conference and said, "I have so little time to be by myself, to stop and think, to exercise—let alone to pray! Where can I find the time?"

Where can *you* find the time to pray?

We can't make more hours in the day, but we can become more skilled in finding ways to connect with God and tap into the blessing of prayer.

What does it start with? Not with a formula, or a rearranged schedule, or a program. It all starts with a new perspective, a clearer vision of the gift, the invitation, and the longevity of prayer, and the amazing power we have in coming to God when life seems to be swirling around us like a tornado.

Let me encourage you: it *is* possible to pray more without changing your job description. You can have a "Mary heart" even when you have a schedule like Martha's. (She was Mary's hard-working sister who Jesus said was distracted about "so many things," much as we are today. See Luke 10:38–42.) For example, my friend Betsy in Rockville, Maryland, starts her day with prayer and exercise.

Betsy—who serves as board president of a private Christian school, is active in her church's women's ministry, leads a weekly neighborhood Bible study in her home, and participates in various other boards and committees—still finds time to pray faithfully for many people and a wide variety of concerns while walking thirty minutes on her treadmill in the basement each morning.

She prays for her husband and sons (including specific Scripture verses she personalizes and prays for them daily) as well as for four families who are very special to her and for the school and women's ministry where her heart really is. Betsy has to drive a lot in the large metropolitan area where she lives, so she keeps a prayer list in her Day-Timer, and every time she gets into the car she prays for someone on the list.

She also prays for the speaker for her church's yearly women's weekend and events, which meant that, before I came to the Fourth Presbyterian Women's Retreat to speak, she'd prayed for me—not just for a week but for months. She prayed for my time with them, for wisdom in what to say, for the book I was working on at that time, for my health and energy. I know Betsy's "treadmill prayers" are effective because I've personally experienced God's answers to them.

You, too, can have an active, growing prayer life, and when you do, you will experience the blessings God promises to those who come to his throne of grace with their needs and burdens. It all starts with your heart and your view of prayer.

That's why this *Busy Woman's Guide to Prayer* begins with a section that celebrates the gift, the invitation, the power, and the longevity of prayer—so we can gain a bigger picture of how God intends prayer to function in our lives before we get down to the nuts and bolts of all the many ways we can integrate it into our daily routines.

A CHANGED PERSPECTIVE

I used to think, *If I don't pray at a certain time of day or in a certain way, my prayers don't really count.* Then my prayer life underwent a radical transformation. I discovered that the apostle Paul's command to continue in prayer means more than just spending a lot of time in prayer; it means sharing a continual dialogue with God wherever I go.

The truth that God listens to my prayers wherever I am didn't sink in until my son Chris left to attend a university that was a twenty-hour drive from home. Oh, how I missed hearing his voice echo around the house and seeing his six-three frame stretched in front of ESPN after he'd finished his homework. Far away on a campus in North Carolina, busy with premed classes, intramural basketball, and studying, Chris didn't call often. But once in a while the phone would ring, and it would be him on the other end of the line. I'd drop everything—the article I was working on, dinner preparations, a load of laundry—just to hear my son's voice.

Now I save my grandkids' voice messages on my cell phone and enjoy replaying them. I have listened again and again to the happy birthday message my son Justin and his little boy, Caleb, left me a few weeks ago, and to my granddaughter Josephine's two-year-old voice saying, "Nandy, thank you for my coloring book and new dress." I never get tired of my daughter Alison calling to say hello, and she lives only four blocks away.

One day I realized God feels the same way about hearing from me, only hundreds of times more so. I'm his child, and so are you (see John 1:12). Whether we're walking, driving across town, rocking a feverish child, or sending a prayer heavenward as we work at the computer, he delights in hearing from us—not just once a day, but throughout the day. Scripture says God "inclines his ear" and is open to hear our prayers (see Psalm 10:17; 40:1; 34:15). Because, you see, we *belong* to him. Psalm 100:3 says, "We are his people, the sheep of his pasture." We are his kids. And God loves to hear *his* children's voices just like I do. That's why he entreats us throughout the Bible to stay in touch with him. "Call to Me," he says in Jeremiah 33:3, "and I will answer you, and I will tell you great and mighty things, which you do not know" (NASB). He wants us to call upon him, to seek him, and to draw near to him (see James 4:8).

I became even more excited about the effects of praying continuously when I noticed that throughout the Bible, God used believers' brief prayers to accomplish great things. It dawned on me that thoughts such as *But I can't pray long enough,* or *If I can't pray one hour, then why pray?* have no biblical basis. It's wonderful to have longer sessions of prayer when I can sit on my sun porch and watch the birds, but remembering that my short prayers can have a big impact encourages me to pray throughout the day.

Whether you're married or single, with or without children, twenty-something or in midlife, you probably struggle with your prayer life as I did with mine. The good news is, you don't have to put either life or prayer on hold. This book will help you build a 24/7 prayer life, starting with the following suggestions.

Praying through Your Busy Day

In the pages ahead, you'll discover that prayer is *integration*, not *separation*; it isn't limited to a slot in your schedule. It's living in the Lord's presence and being open to him. And as you see how prayer releases God's grace and transforming power into your life and those you pray for, you'll find yourself becoming more motivated to pray.

In each chapter of this book you'll find suggestions for practical, doable ways to pray through even your busiest days. I'll start things off here with some of my favorites.

Pray Five Blessings

It *is* possible in only five minutes to really cover a person in prayer and to petition for blessings over his or her life. Let's say your girlfriend Meghan is going on a mission trip to South Africa, and you want to support her in prayer. You can use the letters *B-L-E-S-S* as a springboard to pray for her body, labor, emotional, social, and spiritual needs—and to help you stay focused instead of being derailed by wandering thoughts.[1] Here's how it might work:

Body: "Lord, strengthen Meghan physically on her three weeks in Africa. Grant her safe travel and protection on the whole journey . . ."

Labor: "Father, bless Meghan's efforts as she teaches Bible school to the children in the villages. Bless her labor in assisting in rebuilding the church and working with the medical team . . ."

Emotional: "Help Meghan trust you so completely that she won't be afraid or worried, and so she can sleep peacefully at night . . ."

Social: "Though she's away from her family and friends, help her connect with the others on the mission team. Bring a friend to her so she won't be lonely."

Spiritual growth: "Help Meghan to trust in you, depend on you, and not lean on her own understanding. As she serves others, may she sense your presence in real ways and receive the reward of growing closer to you on this adventure."

Try praying five blessings for five minutes a day for someone or for yourself, and see what God does.

Pray While You Exercise

There is a great parallel between the value of exercise and the value of prayer. When I take time out in the morning (or the afternoon or evening) to walk briskly for thirty to forty-five minutes or to do some strength-training work on machines at the YMCA, the time and effort expended energize me, thus multiplying my productive time and enhancing my life.

The same is true with prayer, only more so. Conversing with God is never wasted effort; it's time well spent. I've found again and again that when we take time to talk and listen to God about our concerns and tasks, he shows us shortcuts and reminds us what really matters. Then we can let the rest go and not be taken captive by the tyranny of the urgent. He gives us solutions to problems and creative ideas we never would have thought of on our own. Time spent in conversation with God renews our youth, energizes our souls, and connects us with the very source of life so we can be a blessing to those around us. What better way is there to spend part of our day?

If you exercise regularly (and I hope you do!), weave your prayer time into your workout. Perhaps you could adapt Betsy's treadmill prayers to the elliptical trainer, Stairmaster, or stationary bike by taping a list of people you want to pray for on the exercise machine. Or follow the lead of my friend Barbara, a busy firefighter and part-time landscaper: she praises God while she stretches to praise music, she prays for her family and friends while she works out in "Body and Soul" classes, and she gives thanks during the cool-down while she takes some much-needed deep breaths.

Get a Good Start

For me, a life of continuous prayer starts each morning, even before I lift my head off the pillow. As soon as I awaken I might say, "Lord, this is the day you've made; help me focus on you in the midst of all I've got to do." Or if I'm tired from being up late the night before and have to get up early the next morning, it might be a short utterance of, "God, I commit the day and myself to you. Grant me the energy I need for today's challenges and tasks."

Get a good start as you begin this book. Say a prayer right now, asking God's Spirit to be your teacher as you read the pages ahead and give you a new vision and perspective of his great gift of prayer—the best thing he ever provided to bless us busy women! This little prayer is an example of how you could jump-start what you have to say to God:

Open my eyes, Holy Spirit, to the gift, the invitation, the power, and the longevity of prayer. May it not be a dry, monotonous duty but a delight as I understand and practice prayer from your point

13

of view. Thank you for being with me as I read the chapters ahead. Help me see that I'm never too busy to pray. Teach me and transform me for your glory and purpose. In Christ's name, amen.

QUESTIONS FOR DISCUSSION OR JOURNALING

Each chapter will end with some questions for small-group discussion or perhaps to inspire you as you journal your prayers and your thoughts about them.

1. Although prayer can be a great source of grace in our lives, at times it almost feels like an obligation, and at other times we feel frustrated about not having enough time to do it. What are your problems or hindrances with prayer? Is it a hectic schedule, not seeing results to your prayers in the past, wondering if God answers prayers, or something else?

2. Which of the busy women described in this chapter do you most relate to? Why?

3. When have you received an answer to prayer or experienced blessings because of somebody else's prayers?

4. Read Jeremiah 33:3. In what area, relationship, or decision do you not know or understand what to do and need guidance from God?

2

The Gift of Prayer

What if God does not demand prayer as much as gives prayer?
What if praying means opening ourselves to the gift of God's own
self and presence? What if our part in prayer is primarily letting
God be giver?

—Martin Smith

Let's look in on the Thorpes, a suburban American family living in Madison, Wisconsin. The two oldest kids—Jessica, thirteen, and Jason, ten—play one or two sports year round. Jessica is on a traveling gymnastics team and plays basketball, field and ice hockey, and soccer in the appropriate seasons. Besides his sports activities, Jason is in Boy Scouts and takes guitar lessons. Joel, the eight-year-old, is active in karate, ice hockey, and drum lessons. All three are on the swim team during the summer, and the two oldest kids sing in the church choir. Luckily, two-year-old Emma is only in a weekly baby gym program, so she still has some time for play.

Mom and Dad practically live on the road, getting the kids where they need to go and trying to make sure they do their homework. Addicted to busyness like lots of people today, the Thorpes find there is little time for family dinners or devotions. Even when they do eat together it's sometimes not until 10 p.m., after one or more of the kids' practice sessions. Mom and Dad Thorpe want the best for their kids, but with both of them working, they find themselves exhausted and irritable when they do have a few minutes to spend with them.

The new status symbol has become not just a bigger house or SUV but an over-packed calendar as well. "*You're* busy? You should see how busy *we* are!" women say to each other. At the same time there's a lot of complaining about being trapped in a frenzied lifestyle. "I feel like I'm on a treadmill, and there's no way to get off," one mom told me.

The hectic lifestyle many parents and kids have today even has a name: experts call it "scheduled hyperactivity," and it leaves little time for family togetherness. A recent research study at UCLA showed that parents and children live virtually apart at least five days a week, and as a result we're scheduling and outsourcing a lot of our relationships, leaving little room for the flow of life.[1] Social-science professors look at American families that are always in motion, strained, and losing intimacy, and warn that if parents and children don't make time for each other to talk and listen, eat together, and enjoy each other's company, emotional ties can wither and die. The biggest destroyer of relationships is *busyness,* leaving relationships fragmented and distant. The heart-to-heart connection that is so desperately needed by children today (and husbands and wives as well) can dissipate without time spent together.

The same thing can happen in our relationship with God.

KNOWING GOD

In addition to all the wonderful blessings it offers us, first and foremost prayer is a *gift*. Not a duty, not an obligation, not another burden or a thing to scratch off our to-do list, but a gift.

A gift worthy of opening and receiving.

Prayer is all about the ongoing discovery of the relationship we have with God our Father through Jesus. It's how we draw near to the Lord, who is infinite yet longs to draw near and be intimate with you and me. As Martin Smith said, prayer means "opening ourselves to the gift of God's own self and presence."[2]

Prayer is how we *know God* instead of just how we know *about* him from what other people say or from filling our minds with knowledge about him. And what could possibly be more important than knowing God personally? Jesus said, "Now this is eternal life: that they may know you, the only true God, and Jesus Christ, whom you have sent" (John 17:3 NIV).

Prayer is also how we *hear God*, really perceive what he is saying to us. It's the opportunity to discover a hidden treasure and how we come to experience his love for us as real and personal rather than simply knowing the verse that says, "God is love" (1 John 4:8).

Prayer is how we hear the beautiful things he wants to do in our life instead of just hearing about what God *used to do* back in Bible days when he parted the Red Sea, healed the multitudes, and performed other miracles. Prayer is discovering the storehouse of blessings the Lord has for us if we will merely come to him and ask.

As Sam Storms said, God is the "Infinite Giver," and "his heart is filled with joy and delight in us, and he loves nothing more than to shower us with gifts that far exceed our capacity to envision or articulate them" (see Ephesians 3:20 and 1 Corinthians 2:9).[3] Scripture says he longs to be gracious and show his mercy to us (see Isaiah 30:18).

In addition to receiving the blessings God wants to give us, prayer is all about relationship. In the same way we get to know anyone else by spending time with him or her, talking and listening so we get to know each other's hearts, prayer is the way to our Father's heart. It's an ongoing dialogue that turns our experience of salvation into a real relationship with the living God as our eternal Father. That's why it's a gift of infinitely great proportions.

One Sunday morning I was trying to explain this concept of prayer to some children in the prayer class I taught for five years in our church. Prayer class was an alternative Sunday school class for kids ages five to twelve, and we had about nine children who chose to attend faithfully. Once in a while, a visitor showed up.

One Sunday, some parents dropped off their three children at the class. First I explained that we were going to pray for flooded villages in Honduras, for the people and particularly for a missionary there. Then I explained to the new children why we were learning and prac-

18

ticing prayer—to know God instead of just knowing about him and to hear God instead of just hearing about him. All I got was a puzzled stare, as if I were speaking Greek. As I pondered a word picture to share with the children, Andrew, an eight-year-old, raised his hand.

"Mrs. Fuller, could I explain to the kids?" he asked.

"Certainly!" I said.

Andrew, who'd been in prayer class for three years, turned to the newcomers and began, "It's kind of like me and President Bush. I've seen him lots of times on the television news. I've read articles about him in the newspaper. I even did a report about him for my social studies project. And I hear his Saturday radio addresses sometimes.

"But I have *never* had a conversation with President Bush. So I don't really know him, do I?"

"No, you don't!" the kids said as the light bulb went on in their heads.

What Andrew said is so true. We can read all kinds of doctrines and information *about* God, and we can watch a religious "expert" expound on theories about God in a television special. But until we have our own conversations and encounters with the Lord, we don't really know him. And if we don't truly know him, how can we love him? How can we possibly know the love he has for us?

As Oswald Chambers once said, "We look upon prayer as a means of getting things for ourselves. The Bible idea of prayer is that *we may get to know God Himself.*"[4] It is the means by which we discover the greatest treasure in all of life.

And where our treasure is, there our heart will be also (see Matthew 6:21).

DUTY OR DELIGHT?

Maybe, like me, you've heard of prayer in the context of Christian disciplines. Often the message taught from pulpits is that prayer is a believer's *duty*, that you are *supposed* to have a daily quiet time with God, that to be a good church member you've got to pray and read the Bible, and that prayer is an obligatory responsibility, a required part of being a Christian.

It is true that many verses of Scripture instruct us to pray, and there are disciplines that help us stay on track spiritually. I certainly value the Christian disciplines. But if that's all we believe about prayer—that it's a duty and obligation—we miss the enormous gift and treasure it brings to our lives. We begin to "feel like hirelings, working our way to heaven through our sacrificial payments of dues as obedient Christians," says Dutch Sheets.[5]

With such a perspective, we'll be guilt ridden, yet no more inspired to pray. If all this book conveys is that prayer is your *duty*, its impact will last only a few days.

However, if we look at prayer from the perspective of love—our love for God and his great love for us—it becomes something else entirely. After all, love is a great motivator.

When Holmes and I met in college and started dating, we didn't think of our getting together as an obligation, something we needed to do once a week. In fact, we looked for all kinds of ways and places to be together. We did laundry together so we could talk. We studied together, though I don't know how much real studying we accomplished. On the weekends we went to movies and parties. We ate together and walked the campus, constantly conversing; we never got tired of each other. That's the way love is.

When I was out of the continental United States for several weeks last year to visit my son, daughter-in-law, and grandbaby, I missed Holmes and the talks we enjoy over coffee in the morning or during dinner at home. Once or twice a day, the phone would ring, and it would be him. Whether I was walking on the beach near my son's house or even when it was late at night due to the five-hour time difference, if it was my husband calling, I didn't think, *Oh, my, this is such a discipline, such a duty to have to talk to Holmes again.*

No, I loved our conversations.

I thanked him for the card he sent me and told him about the spectacular sunset I'd just seen on the beach. I looked forward to hearing what was going on with his work and with the rest of the family, and he wanted to hear what was on my heart, not because somebody told us it was our duty to talk to each other every day, but because we love each other. We have a relationship based on thirty-five years of life together, and when we're apart we miss each other.

Prayer, as Rosalind Rinker described it, is much like that kind of relationship. Prayer "is a dialogue between two people who love each other . . . the expression of the human heart in conversation with God. The more natural the prayer, the more real He becomes."[6] It is a simple but profound definition of the interaction and the gift of prayer as a relationship: walking through my day, thanking God for the hot oatmeal with cranberries and pecans in the morning and for the trees I see in the afternoon that are turning red and gold, sharing my concerns and needs with him before everyone in the household is awake, asking him for patience in bumper-to-bumper traffic, seeking what he wants me to do in a difficult decision, pouring out my heart and my feelings when I'm discouraged or anxious.

Prayer is not a performance; I don't have to speak in spiritual and flowery language and go on and on in a religious-sounding way. I don't have to dry my tears and put on a happy face before talking to my Father either, which is such a relief. I can tell him how I really feel. I can whisper to him if I wake up in the middle of the night, and I can ask him for marching orders when I get out of bed in the morning.

The Gift of Access

To really understand what a gift prayer is, it helps to flash back to the book of Exodus and study those Old Testament days when God's people did not have direct access to the Lord. The reality for thousands of years was that God's people had to stand outside, in the outer court of the temple, away from God's presence and nearness. Only the high priest had the privilege of going into the Most Holy Place on the other side of the veil—which was not a flimsy piece of fabric but a sixty-foot-by-twenty-foot-by-four-inch curtain that was so heavy it took three hundred men to move it! And even then the priest could pass through that veil to God's throne only once a year to minister to the Lord with sacrifices and to pray for the people (see Hebrews 9:3–7).

But everything changed at the cross when Jesus, *our* High Priest, cried out, "It is finished," meaning *complete*, then bowed his head and yielded up his spirit (John 19:30 NIV).

As Alice Smith says, "At the sound of those words, the flesh over his heart ripped in two, redeeming fallen humanity from eternal separation with God. Heaven's windows opened and the hand of God reached the temple tearing the veil in the Holy of Holies from top to bottom. God's heart was forever exposed to all who would seek Him. His heart was open to all who would commune with Him. His throne room was now accessible to all who would enter."[7]

Instead of being excluded outside, away from God's presence and grace, all of us who belong to Christ are welcomed to have relationship and friendship with God, to "come boldly to the throne of our gracious God. There we will receive his mercy, and we will find grace to help us when we need it" (Hebrews 4:16).

This is an incredible thing: each of us is given access to almighty God, who hung the stars and moon in the sky and upholds the entire universe by his very word. We do not have to go through a priest, a prophet, or a minister. We have access to the Lord, not just once a year or on Christmas, Easter, or special occasions, *but twenty-four hours a day, seven days a week, for our whole lives.*

In tragedies such as the attacks on the World Trade Center and the Pentagon or the devastating tsunami in Indonesia, people become desperate to find God. Each week the Wailing Wall in Jerusalem receives thousands of faxes—prayers to God sent from all over the world—that are stuck in the cracks and crevices of the wall. Every day countless people try to e-mail God on the Internet. I heard a brilliant

Ivy League professor say on a prime-time special after 9/11, "If only I could reach God."

But we *can* reach God! And we don't have to send a fax to Israel or seek him via the Internet. God has provided a way through the death and resurrection of Jesus. And in that drawing near to God's throne of grace, we are offered the greatest gift of all: not only the help, grace, and mercy we need for each day and each trial and each difficulty in our lives, but most importantly, intimacy and relationship with God himself.

JOINING JESUS

Two friends, Cindi and Kathy, scrapbook together and make wonderful memories as they share photos and conversation. Susan and I were walking partners for a few years. Karen, Jill, and Jen meet often at Gourmet Yarn Company to talk up a storm and knit beautiful scarves, afghans, and vests. My daughter-in-law Maggie and her friends Emily and Whitney enjoy a relationship that grew by leaps and bounds when they became running partners, training together every morning for a marathon.

Whether it's scrapbooking, knitting, or jogging, when we join someone in what he or she is doing—especially if it's a favorite pastime—a closeness develops, and bonding occurs. It can happen between friends, between a husband and wife, or between a parent and child. When we participate together in the same interest, fellowship and communication naturally flow out of that shared passion.

What has Jesus been doing since he ascended to heaven and sat down in the place of honor at the right hand of the Father? Scripture says he is interceding for us, praying for us day and night; in fact it says he *lives* to make intercession for us (see Hebrews 7:25). When we pray, we are joining Jesus in his full-time, eternal vocation, which brings a mysterious but unmistakable friendship, partnership, and love between us and Christ. It's his life within us that is praying as he lives through us. And through the vehicle of prayer, we draw ever closer into union with Jesus and have the privilege of experiencing his heart of love and compassion for others in intercession.

Who Is God—and Is He Listening?

Unless you believe God wants to bless you, prayer is very difficult. Since prayer involves relationship, how we come to God—or whether we come to him at all—is closely related to how we see or perceive him. As I share in my book *A Fresh Vision of Jesus: Timeless Ways to Experience Christ,* sometimes our view of God and prayer is colored by old attitudes and by impressions of him we got from the kind of father or authority figure who raised us.

Martin Luther, father of the Reformation, described prayer as our heart climbing up into the heart of God. Anne Graham Lotz sees it as a fatherly invitation: "Jesus invites you and me, in his name, to come into his Father's presence through prayer, crawl up into his lap by faith, put our heads on his shoulder of strength, feel his loving arms of protection around us, call him 'Abba' Daddy, and pour out our hearts to him."[8]

But if you had an abusive father, a distant or unloving father, or a dad who expected perfect performance and withheld his affection if you didn't achieve it, then climbing up into God's lap in prayer may not sound very appealing. The father flaws in our lives can obscure our view of God and make us think he doesn't love us or isn't worthy of our trust.

But the truth is, God is the complete expression of love (see 1 John 4:16), and when our vision of him gets cloudy, all we have to do is look to Jesus, the image of the invisible Father, to gain an understanding of him. Hebrews 1:3 says, "The Son is the radiance of God's glory and the exact representation of his being" (NIV).

God is "not a reluctant stranger who must be bullied into responding to the cries and requests of his children," said Sam Storms. "He is not a self-serving tyrant who demands more works and greater deeds before he relents to grant our petitions. . . . Instead, he's an infinitely resourceful God who is never in short supply. He is an infinitely passionate God who rejoices in doing good for those he has redeemed. And he is an infinitely gracious God who abounds in kindness, mercy, and power."[9]

If we know and believe this about God, wouldn't we therefore come boldly and expectantly to his throne of grace?

There is no gift like prayer, for in prayer we find a Father who welcomes us, who listens to us and always understands us; we find peace in the perspective of eternity, strength to hold on and wait for God to work, a haven in his presence, and a safe place to keep those we love.

Praying through Your Busy Day

It's been said that "prayer, the face-to-face, heart-to-heart connection with a God who is on call perpetually—is a gift we unwrap at will."[10] Understanding this gift and having a new attitude about prayer can really revive your spiritual life. Let me encourage you as you go through your busyness today to reflect on prayer as a precious and extraordinary gift from God.

Be Thankful

Say some simple prayers of thanksgiving as you move through your day:

- That God has provided prayer so that we can know God and hear him,
- That prayer is a conversation between two people who love each other—you and the Lord—and you don't have to use fancy or religious words to dialogue with him,
- That the price has been paid to open the way into God's intimate presence,
- For the amazing opportunity to partner with him in his heart and purposes by praying.

Don't Feel Alone

If you feel baffled by the mystery of prayer or burdened by the huge responsibility of prayer requests people give you or inadequate about your abilities or the time you spend in prayer, know you are in good company. This is the case for all of us because, as God's Word tells us, we do not know how to pray. The hope and good news is that God has committed to working within us by his Spirit to teach us to pray (see Romans 8:26). Let me encourage you to pour out these feelings to him. Ask him for help as the disciples did, saying, "Lord, teach us to pray" (Luke 11:1). God's heart is wide open as you seek him.

Catch a Fresh Vision of Jesus

Reflect on how your view of God (either from the father flaws in your life or your present situation) may make prayer difficult. Search the New Testament to better know Jesus (the exact representation of the Father). Begin with Luke 11:11–13, 15:11–32; Matthew 7:11; and John 15:13. Ask God to clean off your filter and help you see him as he really is, the infinitely loving Giver who longs to draw you to himself and be gracious to you.

As you enter into forgiveness for those in your life who misrepresented your loving heavenly Father, and as you open your heart to him, I think you will find, as I have, that coming to him in prayer is a lot more appealing.

Questions for Discussion or Journaling

1. When you think about prayer, is it a duty, a ritual, a responsibility, a burden, or a delight? Do you look forward to it or avoid it?

2. What would our lives be like if we didn't have the gift of prayer at all?

3. What would you have to believe about God to come to him confidently and expectantly when you pray? As I've shared, how we picture God is an important part of whether we turn to him in prayer or run from him—especially in stressful times. What's your image of your heavenly Father? Either draw a picture or write down a few words that come to mind when you think about God. Where did these perceptions come from, and how do they contrast with the way Anne Graham Lotz described prayer?

4. Look up Romans 8:26–27. What does this passage tell about your and my ability to pray?

5. Write in your journal or Day-Timer an insight on prayer from this chapter that has helped you. How could you apply it this week?

3

The Invitation of Prayer

*Prayer with thanksgiving in every care and anxiety and need of
life, is the means that God has appointed for our obtaining
freedom from all anxiety and the peace of God which passes all
understanding.*

—R. A. Torrey

Stirring the marinara sauce, I heard the kitchen phone ring and the
fax machine in my office go off simultaneously. I scrunched my
shoulder to hold the phone as I listened to my friend and layered
lasagna noodles in a casserole dish at the same time. I gasped as she
told me one of our closest friends was in a battered-women's shelter.
The more she talked, the more upset I became. Just then my daughter
called from upstairs, "Mom, I've got to be at field hockey practice in
fifteen minutes, and Chris's basketball game starts in an hour."

Wrapping up the distressing phone call a few minutes later with
promises to stay in touch and see what I could do to help our friend,

I thought, *The fax will have to wait.* I threw another load of clothes into the washer and grabbed my purse and car keys.

As busy as I was on the outside, I couldn't stop the tape inside my head that continually replayed my fears about my friend's downward spiral into alcoholism and her marriage to an abusive husband. I put her at the top of my mental to-do list. Another tape endlessly repeated my worries over our shaky financial situation and my concern over my husband's escalating stress. From the outside, I may have appeared confident and busy that afternoon. In fact, busyness was one of the ways I coped with the worries and fear in my life. But on the inside, it was a different story.

A few nights later I gripped the armrest, white-knuckled, as my husband drove our car on a rain-slick highway to visit our friend at the shelter. "Honey, we might hydroplane if you don't slow down!" I warned. Actually, Holmes is a good driver; I was just an anxious passenger.

A little earlier my mom's CT scan had come back with a suspicious dark spot on her lungs, and I was anxious about her health. My friend's situation in ending up in a battered-women's shelter just added weight to the fifty-pound backpack of burdens I was already carrying. These were real issues and legitimate concerns (except maybe the car anxiety), but my worrying about them wasn't helping one bit. It wasn't solving the problems, and lugging around those concerns was only draining me of the energy I needed to handle *today*.

One morning during this stressful time, I opened my Bible and read, "Therefore humble yourselves [demote, lower yourselves in your own estimation] under the mighty hand of God, that in due time He may exalt you, casting the whole of your care [all your anxieties, all your worries, all your concerns, once and for all] on Him, for He cares for you affectionately and cares about you watchfully" (1 Peter 5:6–7 AMP). I sat there reading the words, letting their impact soak into my heart, and thought, *This is truly the greatest invitation I have ever received.*

I love to get an invitation to a party or be invited to a lunch date with a friend. But to think that Jesus, the Lord of lords and King of kings, was *inviting* me to give him the things that most worried and burdened me—*inviting* me to release my heavy pack of anxieties to him, the Savior who not only was listening and who cared, but who had the power to do something about them—well, it blew me away.

I guess I'd always thought it was just a "girl thing" to worry. I'd assumed it was part of the job description for being a mother. But the more I read in the Scriptures, the more encouragement I found to bring my burdens to the Father through Jesus:

"Do not fret or have any anxiety about anything, but in every circumstance and in everything, by prayer and petition (definite requests), with thanksgiving, continue to make your wants known to God" (Philippians 4:6 AMP).

"Cast your burden on the Lord [releasing the weight of it] and He will sustain you" (Psalm 55:22 AMP).

"Trust in, lean on, rely on, and have confidence in Him at all times, you people; pour out your hearts before Him" (Psalm 62:8 AMP).

Again and again I was struck by what an incredible and gracious invitation this is. These verses tell us that when we take God up on the invitation to cast our cares upon him, he does more than send us a bit of comfort and then go on about his business of running the universe. Instead, the Bible says, when you come to God, weary and burdened, and give him your cares:

- He will give you peace that will guard your heart and mind from panic or anxiety (see Philippians 4:6–9).
- He will sustain you—which means he won't just help you a little, he will give you the perfect measure of grace and strength so the problems won't weigh you down (see Psalm 55:22).
- He will be your "refuge and strength, a very present help in trouble" (Psalm 46:1 KJV; see also Psalm 62:8).

Once you release the situation or person or burden to God, letting go and taking your hands off the problem, then God can really get going. He can intervene, change hearts (including our own), and work things out according to his plan when we stop trying to engineer things ourselves and start trusting him fully.

Learning to Let Go

When Kay Peters and her husband, John, had to decide whether John should accept an invitation to help pastor an Oklahoma church, it was difficult for them, to say the least. To accept the position they would have to move again—after many long separations and moves around the country while he served in World War II and the Korean War and finished his PhD in New England. They would also have to change church denominations, which would cut Kay off from her background. She didn't want any of these changes. But Kay had sensed God saying to her that John should take the position offered to him, and out of obedience, she encouraged John to say yes.

While her husband was in Oklahoma to meet with the church, Kay and her young son, Don, were left behind in New Haven, Connecticut. She struggled with fears and forebodings, knowing that being an assistant pastor would mean lots of routine assignments for John and—worst of all—almost no time with his family. One day she complained, "This might be fine for the youth and the elderly of the congregation. But what about *our* little family? What *we* need is a home life. John and Don, apart so long, need to be together."[1]

Kay spent a good part of that day praying. At 10:00 p.m., weary and at her wit's end, she sat down at the table, buried her head in her arms, and said with exhausted submission, "Father, if we don't have another day of home life, that's no business of mine! That's *Your* business. And if John and Don never have another hour together, that, too, is *Your* business. I'm not going to worry about it any longer. I turn it all over to You."[1]

When those words came out of her heart and her mouth, the peace of God infused Kay, sweeping fear and worry from her.

Relieved of the burden, Kay wondered sleepily why it always took such a prolonged struggle to bring her to complete submission and trust. She went to bed, forgetting all about the job, her home life, and the beauty of father-son relationships. The very next evening John called. He had accepted a position—not as an assistant pastor but as a full-time professor at Oklahoma City University.

When Kay almost shouted, "How did that happen?" her husband explained. "It was strange," he said. "I was ready to sign for the assistant pastorate when I asked if there were any objections to my checking at OCU to see if I could teach there a few hours a week. After all, it seemed a shame to waste the years at Yale."

"Why not?" the pastor responded. So John went out to the college.

There he talked to the president and presented his credentials. "Why, man, we don't want you for a few hours; we want you full time!" the president said.

The church was then persuaded by the university to relinquish its claim, and John became a member of the faculty. "So honey, our worries about a job are over, and we're going to be living where we will all three be happy!" he told her.

God had worked it out in a way they could never have imagined.

John returned to Connecticut and finished his classwork. Then the three of them headed to the Southwest, delighted to be returning to home territory. As a professor, John had more time than he had had in years to spend with his son and wife while he held a position that used his skills and education.[2]

Kay had poured out her heart to God with all her feelings and fears, giving him her requests and turning the whole situation over to the Lord. And he had worked marvelously, doing more than she could have asked or thought. The position in Oklahoma City opened up doors they would have never dreamed of and eventually led them into God's destiny for their lives—the founding of World Neighbors, an organization that has brought clean water, basic health practices, and economic development at a village level to Third World countries around the globe.

THE TOLL OF WORRY

We live in a world that gives us plenty to be burdened about, and news headlines can add to the personal load of problems we're carrying: "West Nile Virus Escalates," "Iran Making Nuclear Weapons," "Inflammation . . . the New Killer," "Mad Cow Disease Taints Beef Supply." Terrorism, job layoffs, and family problems add to our stress. Should I take my hormones or will they cause cancer? Will my daughter be safe, or will violence break out at her high school again?

"Fear is indiscriminate," says Christian writer and speaker Luci Swindoll. "It affects all of us regardless of our age or position in life. Whether our fear is absolutely realistic or out of proportion in our minds, our greatest refuge is Jesus Christ."[3]

Worry can take a huge toll on us. In fact, surveys show that the major mental health issues for women today, both Christian and secular, are fear and anxiety. Yet God invites us again and again to empty out our backpack of troubles and concerns, identify the tapes that replay in our minds by day and keep us up at night—and give them all to him.

When my daughter Alison was in England for a college mission trip, she asked my future daughter-in-law Maggie and me to come with her and travel around Europe via Eurail train after the mission trip was complete. I tried to pack light for the almost-three-week journey through five countries, but I always have a tendency to take too much, even for a weekend trip. We each took a backpack and a small, rolling suitcase; I was confident at the start of the trip that mine wasn't too heavy.

But by the time we'd dragged our luggage to and from airports and train stations and up and down steep flights of stairs to get on the trains and to get to our hotel rooms, I was so worn out I wanted to throw both my bags in the nearest river. That's the way it is with carrying our burdens. "Worrying doesn't take away tomorrow's grief," said Corrie ten Boom. "It takes away today's strength. It does not enable us to avoid evil, but it makes us incapable of dealing with it when it comes."[4]

As busy women, we carry a lot of things. Some of us carry a briefcase holding our computer and business papers; others carry a teacher's tote bag packed with papers to grade at home after hours of work at school. Some carry a full diaper bag. Lots of us carry grocery bags. Others of us have a duffel bag to carry our workout gear to the gym. When I go back and forth between my office and home, I carry books, files, my laptop computer, and my purse.

We carry so many things, but one thing we *don't* need to be carrying is our burdens. Jesus invites us to give them all to him. And it's not something we do only once—"Oh, I gave God my sins and guilt at salvation, and I gave him my burdens last week!"—but continuously, in an ongoing way. Because even if we solve all our problems today and life goes smoothly for a few days, we're probably going to face a new burden or trouble around the corner that could weigh us down.

This is a very current and ever-deepening truth for me. Maybe because I'm a slow learner or a born worrier, but also because I am human. Just last night I was so weary. I had been sick with a respiratory virus all weekend but had made it to an event I had to speak at on Saturday, so by nine o'clock Sunday night I was exhausted. My husband had left again for his five-day work week in another city, and I was alone.

As I got down on my knees in my bedroom, many situations were heavy on my mind: my concern for Holmes and how tired he'd seemed all weekend; it was taking him a long time to recover from a recent bout of bronchitis. Whether the two old cars would sell so we could pay for the apartment we'd rented for him in Dallas. All the logistics of moving into the apartment and yet keeping up our house in Oklahoma. The overwhelming tasks I was facing in the next few months and how I was going to get everything done this week and help take care of our two-year-old grandson while his mom was out of town. Even small things like who I could find to care for our dog while I was at an out-of-town speaking engagement.

The list went on and on, and I felt crushed under the weight of it all. I knew in my head that Jesus had told me not to worry, to let him handle my burdens, but actually doing it is something I have to work at in my life again and again.

Then, as I sank to my knees, his wonderful words came to me,

"Come to me, all you who are weary and burdened" (I definitely qualified!), "and I will give you rest. Take my yoke upon you and learn from me, for I am gentle and humble in heart, and you will find rest for your souls. For my yoke is easy and my burden is light" (Matthew 11:28–30 NIV).

I love how *The Message* renders that passage: "Are you tired? Worn out? . . . Come to me. Get away with me and you'll recover your life. I'll show you how to take a real rest. Walk with me and work with me—watch how I do it. Learn the unforced rhythms of grace. I won't lay anything heavy or ill-fitting on you. Keep company with me and you'll learn to live freely and lightly."

One by one, I laid my burdens at Jesus's feet, and I did find rest in my soul, knowing I could trust him with these concerns so I could go to bed and get some much-needed sleep. Tomorrow would be another day and Jesus has told us, "Do not worry about tomorrow, for tomorrow will worry about itself. Each day has enough trouble of its own" (Matthew 6:34 NIV). Though the issues were definitely not solved yet, as I pulled the covers over my head, I knew the Lord who never slumbers or sleeps could handle them.

God's gracious invitation to cast our cares on him isn't a one-time invitation. It's offered to us day by day, moment by moment, so we can live in freedom rather than fear, have energy rather than be depleted by worry, and draw on his perfect measure of grace and strength for every problem we face in life.

FINDING INTIMACY

For many of us—especially for us busy, self-reliant, Type A women— coming to God with our burdens isn't easy. We have believed and followed the adage that "God helps those who help themselves." Contrary to popular opinion, that verse is *not* in the Bible.

But the truth is, if we really want to find intimacy and closeness in our relationship with God, we need to respond to his invitation. We need to give him our load of worries and stop carrying it all ourselves. In his book *Pierced by the Word,* John Piper said something so insightful about this need: "One of the reasons we don't know God deeply is that we don't venture much on His pledge to carry things for us. Knowing God with a sense of authentic, personal reality is not merely a matter of study. It is a matter of walking with Him through the fire and not being burned. It is a matter of not being crushed under a load because He carries it for you at your side."[5]

Christ, who has carried our sin, pledges to carry our anxieties and burdens, Piper says. Every one of them. All our lives. Not so that we can lie around, watch reality shows, and ignore our responsibilities. But *so we'll be more fruitful.*

In the parable of the farmer and the seeds in Luke 8, Jesus warns us not to be consumed with the cares of this world because those worries are like weeds that will choke out the Word, letting our lives become unfruitful and unproductive. He put worry on a par with worldly behavior, saying, in effect, "Don't let your hearts be weighed down with carousing and drunkenness and the cares of this life." As we give the Lord our worries and cares, our roots go down deeper in him with every trial, and we become like "the seed in the good earth—these are the good-hearts who seize the Word and hold on no matter what, sticking with it until there's a harvest" (Luke 8:15 MSG).

We can entrust every loss, every trial, every task, every problem and anxiety to the Lord, who will sustain us and carry us all the days of our lives.[6] What an incredibly freeing truth and gracious invitation!

Even when our burden is heavier and more urgent than anything we've ever faced, God's invitation still stands. My friend Cecilia's son Jake was sent to Iraq in a combat unit as a machine gunner last spring during some of the most violent weeks of the war. When news reports showed soldiers dying or Humvees being blown up by roadside bombs, fear threatened to overwhelm Cecilia. But she found a wonderful way to remind herself of Jesus's invitation to carry her burdens. She put a framed picture of Jesus up on her wall, and whenever she felt worried about Jake and his Marine platoon, she wrote the specific need or concern on a yellow sticky note and put it up on the picture of Jesus—symbolizing her giving that concern to him.

When she woke up in the middle of the night, fearful about the possibility of her son being hit by mortars or rocket-propelled grenades (RPGs) or suffering in the 140-degree heat, she gave those concerns to Jesus. As the weeks of Jake's deployment went on, more and more sticky notes were stuck to the picture of Jesus until it was almost covered with Cecilia's fears and burdens about her son and his fellow Marines. The biggest note was on a full-size piece of paper that said, "Lord, watch over Jake's battalion, and let there be no losses or bad injuries in their unit!"

When Cecilia felt afraid, he exchanged her panic for his peace.

One night God gave her a mental picture of Jake, in his machine-gun vehicle, surrounded by huge, protective wings. The image came from Psalm 91, especially verse 4, which says, "He will shield you with his wings. He will shelter you with his feathers. His faithful promises are your armor and protection." Cecilia asked an artist friend to sketch this image, then she copied it onto cards, laminated them, and sent them to Jake and all the Marines in his platoon to keep in their pockets.

Amazing things happened in that platoon. For example, an RPG landed in one Marine's lap, but he was able to throw it out of the vehicle before it exploded, and a huge rocket exploded right near her son and a group of his buddies, yet no one was injured. Jake and every man in his unit came home safely.

He and his fellow Marines are now on another tour of duty in Iraq. They are in the midst of ever-present danger, and several in the unit have been wounded or killed. While Cecilia knows that God doesn't always answer our prayers the way we hope he will, she's assured that he promises to be with us—and our loved ones— through whatever lies ahead. And that security gives her peace from worry. Cecilia knows Jesus will be waiting with open arms to receive and carry her concerns, no matter what they are.

PRAYING THROUGH YOUR BUSY DAY

Henri Nouwen suggested that we make a conscious choice to "move the attention of our anxious heart away from the waves (of troubles or feelings of fear or pity) to the One who walks on waves and says, 'It's me. Don't be afraid.'" When our thoughts drift back to our worries, we can center our minds on the words of the Lord's Prayer, the Twenty-third Psalm, or other familiar scriptures.[7] Here are some other ways you can take God up on his invitation to carry your burdens.

Post Your Prayers

A physical symbol of giving your cares to Jesus—like Cecilia's practice of writing her worries on sticky notes and putting them on Jesus's picture—can really be helpful. My friend Patty Johnston used a similar idea when word got out that she was a faithful intercessor and she began getting an overwhelming number of prayer requests. *What am I going to do about prayer? Why am I so burdened down with all these needs?* she wondered. Through her inner dialogue with the Lord, she began to relax, remembering that God would be doing most of the work, that he was able to do so, and that she was simply to make the request.

That's when he gave her the idea for "Post-it note prayers." Whenever a friend calls with a prayer request, Patty might pray with that person on the phone, then she writes out the prayer on a Post-it and sticks it inside her prayer closet, a cabinet in her kitchen especially designated for prayer needs. When it's a heavier matter, she lights a candle to remind her to pray about the request throughout her day. Every year or two Patty takes down the Post-it note prayers she's brought to God and stores them in a container in the closet. As she looks through them, it's amazing how many have been marvelously answered.

What could you designate for holding prayer requests you entrust to God, as Patty did her "prayer closet"? It could be as simple as a notebook, an inner kitchen cabinet, or a "God box." Its role is to remind you to leave the need with the Lord and also to be a source for thanksgiving as you look back and see how he worked.

Light a Candle

For centuries lighting candles has been part of prayer in Christian churches and individual lives. Just as Patty found, the candle, a symbol of Christ's light and of hope, can be a reminder to keep praying for the person and to remind you that you have already given the request to God so you don't have to help him "fix" things in your own way. Every time you pass the candle, you can say, "Thank you, Lord, that you are well able to handle this difficult situation, and for what you're going to do."

Be Specific and Honest

When you cast your cares on Jesus, be specific. Instead of just saying, "Lord, I give you all my burdens. Amen," tell him honestly what you're asking him to carry. "In other words, unload on him," says Lynne Hammond in *Secrets to Powerful Prayer*.

When I read those words I thought of how, when my daughter

"unloads" on me, she doesn't just say it's been a bad day. She pours it all out: how tired she is, how badly her rash caused by the shingles is itching and how miserable it makes her feel, how her toddlers are trying her patience and she needs a break *soon*.

"That's exactly the way you should cast your cares upon the Lord," says Hammond. "You stop trying to sound all nice and spiritual, and you have a conversation with God and tell him everything that's been worrying you."[8]

Pray . . . and Release

When I met Leslie, she told me that when her preschool daughter, Marlie, was to have open-heart surgery for a congenital heart defect, she couldn't pray at all for several weeks because she knew that if she prayed, she had to release Marlie to God. She asked everyone else to pray for her daughter's healing. But the thought of the risks, of seeing her little daughter being wheeled into an operating room where she couldn't go, and of Marlie's little heart being stopped to operate on it overwhelmed her; she was too numb and too angry to pray.

It was a tug of war—God pulling on one side, Leslie on the other.

"Let her go; I'll catch her," God promised.

"I can't . . . I don't want to lose her. What if you *don't* catch her?" Leslie responded.

Finally she realized that although she couldn't guide the doctor's hands during surgery, God could; she knew he was trying to reach her and wanted her to take a leap of faith. Finally God tugged again, and Leslie let go and fell into his arms. Yielding her fears, she entrusted her daughter to the Lord and prayed fervently for her. A peace began to replace the pervasive fear. When the day arrived for them to meet with one of the doctors for the pre-surgery appointment, the physician examined the echocardiogram (the picture of Marlie's heart) and said, "That hole is really small. This one looks pretty small too." Finally the physician looked at Leslie and her husband and said, "I'll send this video to the surgeon, but it looks to me like she'll never require heart surgery; her heart is practically normal."

Marlie's heart was healed, and so was her mom's. When she took that difficult leap of faith, God was there to catch her. And regardless of the outcome in the burdens you face, he will be there for you too.

Meditate on the Go

A woman with many responsibilities can meditate on God's Word throughout her day. As Edith Schaeffer explained, "All the day long, as I walk in fields or city streets, as I sit at the typewriter or make a bed with fresh sheets, as I converse with professors or tiny eager human beings wanting to learn . . . as I work in a lab or scrub a floor all day long in office or factory, I can meditate upon the Law, the Word of God, which my eyes have read or my ears have heard or my fingers have felt in Braille."[9]

Write out the following scriptures on separate index cards and memorize them so they'll run through your mind during the day, encouraging you to release your burdens to God: Philippians 4:6–9, Matthew 6:34, Matthew 11:28, Psalm 62:8, and Psalm 55:22.

Questions for Discussion or Journaling

1. What is your greatest burden or concern, the thing that wakes you up in the night or the problem that weighs you down during the day?

2. What are some of the personal cues you experience when you're afraid or anxious? What do you do or experience when you're chronically worried about something? Insomnia? Getting caught up in a frenzy of busyness? Controlling others, etc.?

3. What is an area of your life where you would like to experience more peace and less anxiety? Could you pray about this and release it to God?

4. Read Isaiah 41:10–14. How does this passage apply to any of the situations mentioned above that push your panic button? In the midst of this fear-filled world, what is God saying to you in this Scripture passage?

5. Read the wonderful promise in Psalm 146:8. What is God saying to you about his desire to help you when you are overwhelmed or burdened?

4

The Power of Prayer

Around us is a world lost in sin,
above us is a God willing and able to save;
it is ours to build the bridge that links
heaven and earth, and prayer is the
mighty instrument that does the work.
If we do our part, God will do His.
—E. M. Bounds

A WOMAN NAMED MONICA persevered in prayer for more than nineteen years for her wayward son, and when he was converted he became one of the great fathers of the Christian church. As a result of John Knox's relentless prayers and life, most of Scotland turned to Christ.

A British missionary named Anne prayed and followed where God sent her, although the work was perilous and her safety was uncertain. Because of her courage, her devoted prayers, and her work in sharing the gospel through many years of ministry, many Chinese people came to know Christ.

For two years a nine-year-old Virginia girl named Hope prayed daily for Mongolia, and soon the greatest spiritual awakening in history began to unfold there. Whereas in 1989 there were believed to have been only four Christians in all of Mongolia, today the number of believers is thirty thousand—and growing.

We've seen that prayer is a great gift and an extraordinary treasure because it's all about knowing God. And it's our response to a matchless invitation that urges us to give him our burdens and worries. Even if those things were all we knew and experienced of prayer, it would be more than valuable enough to invest our time in.

But there is more.

One of the marvelous things about prayer is that God not only hears our prayers but answers them in miraculous ways. Prayer is the source of heaven-sent power, and its possibilities are limitless. It is the conduit through which God's power, grace, and light are released into a dark world. Long ago Chinese theologian Watchman Nee said, "Our prayers lay the track down on which God's power can come. Like a mighty locomotive, his power is irresistible, but it cannot reach us without rails." Now there are much greater forms of power than locomotives, but the principle is just as true today. Nothing is more powerful than prayer because our prayers lay the tracks and prepare the way for God's mighty power to be released on earth. Prayer forms the bridge between earth's need and heaven's unending supply of grace.

And whether it's an atheist coworker you're praying for, a family member whose life is a mess, a fearful neighbor down the street, a local school your kids attend, a nation thousands of miles away, or your own personal need, God shows up and works when his people pray. I believe the prayers of women today are God's secret weapon to bring his presence and power into a dark world desperate for his mercy and help.

GOD WORKS AS WE PRAY

When I was in Thailand on a ministry trip, I met a missionary whose experience reminded me how God works when we lay the tracks in prayer, wherever that is and no matter what the obstacles. My husband, our missionary friend Paula, and I had just taken a prayer walk around the largest Buddhist temple in northern Thailand, and nothing seemed to happen while we were there. I wondered whether those prayers we uttered as we walked the one thousand steps up to the temple and around its massive golden statues really mattered.

But later, when I heard what God did in Laos, I was encouraged and reminded that God often works behind the scenes, where we can't initially see. A woman named Jan and six other missionary women from Chiang Mai in northern Thailand went on a prayer walk in northern Laos. As they traveled into the country, they heard about nineteen Laotian men who were imprisoned for their faith— jailed just for loving and serving Jesus. The women asked God if there was something they could do to encourage and pray for those pastors, and they felt prompted to find the prison.

When they finally arrived there, it proved to be a huge, formi- dable barracks-type cement building surrounded by wire fences. The women could not go inside the prison and perhaps wondered for a moment why God had sent them there. Then they sensed they were to begin walking around the perimeter of the prison, praying and singing very loudly. They weren't sure if their voices could be heard on the inside because the thick concrete walls of the building looked impenetrable. But they kept asking God, in his way of doing things, to please minister to the Christian men imprisoned behind those walls. The Spirit led the women to sing hymns they thought the men might recognize, and they continued to pray, sing, and walk for an hour before moving on to their next destination.

About six months later, one of the Laotian pastors was released, and he told this story: "One day I was let out of my cell like we were each day for five minutes to get our food ration. The guards called me over and said, 'Hey, come here. Listen to this crazy group of women singing.' When I came closer I heard them singing 'How Great Thou Art,' and I knew Jesus hadn't forgotten us."

Amazingly, God had the women there prayer-walking and singing during this man's *five-minute window* outside his cell so he could be reminded that God was with him and that he was on God's heart. The men had been persecuted and imprisoned for their faith, and at times they may have felt depressed or forgotten. Yet the women's footsteps and prayers paved the way for God to deliver much-needed hope and strength to them. With his soul renewed, the pastor was able to go back and encourage his brothers in Christ inside the walls so that they could continue to stand for their faith.

OUT OF DARKNESS

One thing I love about prayer is that it doesn't matter how old or young you are or whether you've had seminary training or are a new believer. The simple truth is that God works powerfully when his people pray—because it's all about the Lord and his power and plans, not about our degrees, qualifications, or eloquence. It's not about how long or short a time we've known God. Our prayers are merely a conduit, but they form a vital link.

An Oklahoma City woman told me about her five-year-old grandson Jace, who was visiting his grandfather in the hospital. The family had gathered around the grandfather's bed for what doctors said would be the last time they would see him alive. Moving to the corner of his grandpa's room, Jace said, "Grandma, what's wrong with Grandpa?"

"Honey, he's very sick," she answered.

Jace said very loudly, "Oh, God, send down your big hand and heal my grandpa, right now!"

Overhearing Jace's words, the family members remaining around the bed said, "Amen!"

To their great surprise, within the hour the elderly man had come out of the coma. His vital signs returned to normal, and in a few days he was released from the hospital. He lived for three more months, and during that time he committed his life to Christ for the first time. His eternal destiny was changed by the prayers of the youngest member of the family.

Prayer is our greatest resource for hearts to be changed and spiritual eyes to be opened. We can tell people the truth, we can teach them and train them if they're our children or in our Sunday school class, but we cannot change their hearts. Trying to change someone's heart, maybe because he or she is careening down a destructive path, is a frustrating business at best, and often results in the opposite of what we hope for: the person becomes more resistant. God is the only One who, by his Spirit, can change and transform a human heart—turning the person from darkness to light. And his heart-changing power is released when we pray.

A wonderful example of this power is the story I heard about four single women who moved to inner-city Detroit for their new jobs. They thought it would be fun to live in the urban part of the city, so they moved into an apartment together, excited about the changes and new opportunities offered in the big city. What they didn't know was that they'd moved into a neighborhood that was terrorized by gangs and crime.

Discovering this, they decided instead of breaking their lease and moving out they would develop their home into a house of prayer for their neighborhood and especially for the young people. From then on, one evening a week the women gathered to pray that the teenagers in the gangs would come out of darkness and into the light of Christ.

As they kept praying, God was working behind the scenes. A few weeks into their weekly prayer meetings, the young women heard that four teenagers had left one of the gangs. That night they prayed specifically for those four young people. Then they felt led to go to the teens' apartment and share the good news of Jesus with them. As they sat on the floor with the teenagers, the four former gang members gave their lives to Christ. The next Sunday the young women took them to their church to begin Bible study and discipleship. In the months that followed, those four teens began to grow in God's Word and reach out to the other youth of the neighborhood.

Before long, they were bringing other former gang members to church. Gradually the atmosphere of the whole community began to change. No longer were people terrorized by the teens' crimes or by violence in the streets. God had used the prayers of four young, single girls to change a neighborhood and bring people out of the kingdom of darkness and into the kingdom of God's light.

When teachers pray, God works mightily in their classrooms. In fact, he does some of his best work in the darkest, most unlikely places. A third-grade teacher's public-school class was filled with kids from single-parent or dysfunctional families, kids who were undernourished and neglected, and kids who had been beaten or raped by other members of their family. One child's dad had died of AIDS; another parent was in prison. The teacher's heart bled for these children.

Before the school year started, she and her husband went to her classroom, and together they prayed over every single desk in the room. They prayed that God would place an angel behind each child throughout the coming year to watch over and protect him or her.

About a month after the school year began, the teacher assigned her students to write about what they would like to be when they grew up. Everybody was busily writing away when Andrew raised his hand. When she asked what he needed, he asked her how to spell the word *mighty*. She told him then asked why he needed to know. Andrew said it was because when he grew up, he wanted to be a "mighty man of God."

When Andrew said this, Mark, the kid who sat next to him, asked, "So what's a mighty man of God?" The teacher, swallowing back her tears and knowing she couldn't say anything in the class-room, told Andrew to go ahead and tell Mark what it was.

"It's a man who puts on the armor of God and is a soldier for God," Andrew explained.

After listening to the conversation between the two boys, the teacher, with a big lump in her throat, started to walk back to her desk. But Andrew motioned with his finger for her to come closer. He whispered to her, asking if she believed in angels. After telling him yes, he asked her if she thought people could see angels, and she said she thought some people probably could.

Andrew said that he could see them. In fact, he said, he could see an angel standing behind each child in the room.

Prayers That Reach Across the Ocean

An elderly woman shared with me how the power of prayer can reach a continent away, across an ocean, when a mother's love is connected with God's love through intercession.

Dorothy's three sons all served in World War II, but she was most concerned about the youngest, Jack. Though he was from a devout Christian family, he'd started hanging out and drinking with a wild bunch of guys in their southern town. A dedicated believer, Dorothy grew increasingly worried that her son might be developing an alcohol problem, and she was heartbroken when she saw his heart turning more to the world than to God.

When Jack got his orders to ship out for Germany, his mother was wracked with anxiety, overhearing Jack tell his brothers he couldn't wait to taste the German beers. Every day during the war, Dorothy prayed for her sons. But her continual prayer for Jack, in addition to asking for his safety and protection, was, "Oh, Lord, may every glass of beer he tries taste like bitter gall."

This was a determined woman who never stopped praying for her son. Though she received only a few letters from him in the four years he was in Europe, none encouraged her about his spiritual state.

But one day, after the war was over, Jack came home. He walked in the door, threw his arms around his mama, and gave her the biggest hug she'd ever gotten. She sat him down to a home-cooked lunch, and they began to talk. Jack shared some of his experiences in combat and in different parts of Germany where he had served.

"The strangest thing that happened, though, Mom," he explained, "was that every time I tried a different kind of German beer—and I tasted every type of beer I could get my hands on while I was there—they all tasted just like bitter gall. I kept trying them as I visited bars and beer gardens, but those countless steins of German beer tasted so bad I couldn't drink them."

Dorothy got out her prayer journal and showed Jack what she had asked God to do every day he was away, keeping him safe in combat but also safe from the harmful influences of alcohol. Through prayer, the "divinely devised means of releasing God's heavenly powers upon the earth,"[1] a young man felt the power of his mother's prayers though he was hundreds of miles away from her direct influence.

In fact, Jack was so amazed at God's power, that on that very day he gave his life to God and eventually became a pastor who served the Lord faithfully the rest of his life.

God Works in Switzerland

I have personally experienced the power of women's prayers when I've ministered at women's retreats, but one of the most memorable examples of this power occurred when I traveled to Switzerland and France to speak. Although most of the events were sponsored by Christian groups or churches, I received one invitation from an international women's group, a secular organization of expatriate women from many countries who live in Switzerland because of their husbands' jobs or their own careers.

In the summer before the event, Leslie, one of the group's board members, and a few other Christians in the group began praying earnestly that God would touch the hearts of the women through my message. But when the association's leadership realized I was a Christian, they put strict limitations on what I could say. They chose the topic of "The Gift of Encouragement" but said there could be no talk of God, no mention of prayer, and no Bible verses given in my message. Leslie and her friends prayed on, and we joined them as well.

When we arrived that September day at the downtown building where the association had its suite of offices, I was greeted by the president, who immediately told me we couldn't sell my books (although they'd invited me to bring them as resources to offer the women). Instead, she said, my husband would be allowed to display the books on a back table.

After being introduced, I began sharing my message on how the women could encourage their children, friends, and family—minus Scripture verses and Christian references, as they had insisted.

All of a sudden, as I was speaking, I sensed God's Spirit move throughout the room, almost like the tide coming in at the shore of the ocean, opening and melting the hearts of those very well-dressed, international women. The Lord's love seemed to flow among the rows of women, and many dabbed away tears that welled up in their eyes. Afterward, women lined up to tell me how touched they were by the message. Many shared how desperate they were for encouragement because they received so little of it from their husbands, and several of them said their children were rarely encouraged by their teachers (it wasn't the Swiss style of motivating students). A number of the women opened up and shared personal problems and asked me to pray for them. Then the president came up and said, "We've changed our minds. Our members are saying they want your books, so you may autograph them after all."

But that wasn't the end of it. Although the few Christian women in the organization had tried for several years to get the board to include Bible study as one of the myriad activities offered by the club, the request had always been refused. The night after I spoke, several women called the new president-elect and told her they wanted to have a Bible study. What a huge breakthrough!

It wasn't that I had spoken sterling words of change that day but that the power of God had come on the wings of those intercessory prayers sent up by Leslie and the other praying friends. Those prayers had opened the club members' hearts to God's love. James 5:16 says, "The earnest (heartfelt, continued) prayer of a righteous man [or, I might add, *woman*] makes tremendous power available [dynamic in its working]" (AMP).

God's mysterious power is irresistible and unfathomable, and our prayers are needed to prepare the way for it.

Prayer Shapes History

"Prayer is the means by which the MUCH MORE of God becomes ours in daily living," says Jack Taylor. "There is no other way. Let the average Christian wake up to the MUCH MORE of prayer and his life can never be the same again," says Jack Taylor. "Prayer binds the devil and his bands of demons; prayer unleashes the powers of heaven and releases the angelic hosts to do their work in ministering to the heirs of salvation. Prayer bombards the spiritual targets of the devil until he is forced to give up and retreat. Prayer blesses God and God's children. Prayer is our becoming one with God. Prayer changes the destinies of nations and sets men free."[2]

Derek Prince and his wife, Lydia, and their eight adopted daughters experienced this truth in a very vivid way. They were living in Jerusalem in 1948 when the UN declared the creation of the new, independent state of Israel. All the Arab countries in the region were incensed, and on the inauguration date of the new state they declared war. It was a David-and-Goliath situation. Like the shepherd boy with only a few stones and a sling, the 650,000 Jews had very little ammunition, food, or supplies, and they faced attacks by the fifty-million-strong hostile Arab armies, which had massive military resources at their disposal.

Prince's wife had seen battles before in her twenty years of living in Jerusalem, but this one looked like it would be devastating for the Jewish people. Every day Lydia and Derek searched God's Word for direction and hope, and for guidance in how the Lord wanted them to pray. As they read, they became convinced it was God's plan to restore the nation of Israel, and they were inspired to pray that the Jews wouldn't be destroyed by the attacking Arabs.

One day, as they were praying, Derek heard Lydia say a brief prayer petitioning God to simply "paralyze the Arabs." Their home was near the front lines, and the family was living in the basement during the first six weeks of combat. Since the Israeli army had set up an observation post in their backyard, they had gotten to know many of the soldiers. During the UN-imposed cease-fire, some of the soldiers told the couple about the first weeks of the fighting.

"There's something we can't understand. We go into an area where the Arabs are dominating. They outnumber us ten to one and are much better armed than we are. Yet, at times they seem powerless to do anything against us. *It's as if they are paralyzed!"* said one soldier.[3]

Although the fierce fighting continued, the invading Arab armies were eventually defeated, and the state of Israel became strongly established. God's Word in a woman's prayer did not return void but accomplished his purpose and plan. And this family got to hear and see firsthand how the Lord had used their prayers to shape history in a crucial time in the life of the nation of Israel.

Praying through Your Busy Day

Often we think it's our work and our efforts that will make the most impact in bringing success or needed changes. But understanding that prayer is the major work and thus the most productive use of our time makes a huge difference. The enemy doesn't want us to pray because he doesn't worry about our prayerless work, prayerless parenting, or prayerless self-efforts; on the other hand when everything we do is bathed in prayer, he has a real problem! The prayers of even the weakest, youngest, poorest, least influential, or newest believer who is right with God through a relationship with Jesus Christ can pierce the darkness. Keep this powerful truth in mind as you consider these ideas for saturating the components of your busy life in prayer.

Bathe Women's Events in Prayer

I can literally sense the difference when I speak at a women's retreat that has been bathed in lots of prayer, and one that hasn't. There's an old saying that explains it:

> Much prayer, much blessing.
> Little prayer, little blessing.
> No prayer, no blessing.[4]

It's so important to pray for our conferences and other events: pray that the women's hearts will be open to the truth, that God's Word will penetrate their hearts, that there will be lasting transformation and not just a weekend mountaintop feeling, that the speaker will hear God clearly and communicate his message effectively.

Even the great apostle Paul asked people to pray for his work in communicating God's truth. "Pray that I'll know what to say and have the courage to say it at the right time," he asked (Ephesians 6:19 MSG). He begged believers to pray so God's Word would "simply take off and race through the country to a groundswell of response" (2 Thessalonians 3:1 MSG). The next time your women's ministry plans an event, I encourage you to gather a team of women who like to pray and who believe God is able to answer prayers. Write down what you want to see the Lord do, then pave the way by praying.

Take the Step to Trust God Completely

O. Hallesby said, "When humanity fell into sin, our souls were not only cut off from God, but the whole wiring system was destroyed. To restore it, Jesus had to suffer and die. The wiring is now in order again. We may all re-establish contact with, and make use of, the powers of the heavenly world. And prayer is the mysterious little instrumentality whereby the contact is made, enabling the powers of his salvation to reach our souls, and our bodies, and through us, to others, as far as our zeal and perseverance will permit." Hallesby also described prayer simply as letting Jesus come into our hearts.[5]

God has given us the potential to know him and his power; he has blessed us with the ability to talk to the One who created us, knows us, and loves us. But the first step or condition of experiencing this power is to get right with God or, as the Bible says, to be reconciled to God our Father through Jesus Christ. This opens our heart and life to all that he's planned for us and welcomes his Spirit to live within us.

To take this all-important step, you could simply pray something like this: "Lord Jesus, I believe that you died for me. I know I have sinned, and I am asking for your forgiveness. I give myself to you. I want to stop running my own life and give over the controls to you, to know you and walk with you through all of life. Thank you for saving me. Thank you for forgiving me. Thank you for loving me. Amen."

This prayer is just a suggestion. Please know that the important thing isn't that you pray exactly the right words; it's that your heart turns to God in whatever way he leads you. It is by his grace, not by our works, that we are brought into relationship with him. The apostle Paul wrote, "God saved you by his special favor when you believed. And you can't take credit for this; it is a gift from God. Salvation is not a reward for the good things we have done, so none of us can boast about it. For we are God's masterpiece. He has created us anew in Christ Jesus, so that we can do the good things he planned for us long ago" (Ephesians 2:8–10).

The wonderful news is that as you continue in this new life, it will be his mighty power at work within you and through your prayers, and "he is able to accomplish infinitely more than we would ever dare to ask or hope" (Ephesians 3:20).

Enlarge Your Circle of Prayer

Maybe you aren't a parent in the traditional sense, but like the teacher who prayed for angels to watch over each of her students, you may be a teacher or coach or youth leader to a group of kids. Or maybe you're an aunt or a close friend of a family with children. Aunts can have an incredible impact on their nieces and nephews by praying for them. Teachers, coaches, friends, and youth leaders can make an eternal difference in the lives of "their" young people through prayer.

Increase your circle of prayer; widen your perspective of who "your" children are. The greatest investment you can make in your own life, in the lives of those you love, and in those who share your church, school, and neighborhood is "to intercede for them in prayer. . . . What no amount of human effort, ingenuity, or preaching could ever accomplish, God can do, and he will do it in response to our prayers."[6]

QUESTIONS FOR DISCUSSION OR JOURNALING

1. If you really believe that prayer is the greatest, most valuable work you can do, how can this change your spiritual life or your use of time?

2. What is an area of your life where you've experienced the power of prayer, either in praying for yourself or for someone else?

3. Hannah Hurnard once said, "Prayer changes us and therein lies its glory and its purpose." Prayer is immensely powerful, but perhaps one of the greatest ways God works is to change us, the pray-ers. When have you felt changed (perhaps in your attitude, behavior, or motive) as you were praying for someone or some circumstance?

4. In what situations, relationships, or problems do you truly need God's power at this time? Read Matthew 18:19–20 and then partner with a friend or your small-group members to lift up your situation and ask God to work in it and in you through the power of his Spirit.

5

The Longevity of Prayer

The story of your life will be the story of prayer and answers to prayer. The shower of answers to prayer will continue to your dying hour.

Nor will it cease then. And when you pass out from beneath the shower, your dear ones will step into it. Every prayer and sign which you've uttered for their future welfare will, in God's time, descend upon them as a gentle rain of answers to prayer.

—O. Hallesby

We all love to see the answers to prayer, and I have found that the more I pray, the more I see and experience God working in the world around me. I love the way O. Hallesby, the Norwegian prayer theologian, used a word picture to articulate this truth: "The longer you live a life of prayer, the more answers to prayer you will experience," he said in his classic book *Prayer*. "As white snow flakes fall quietly and thickly on a winter day, answers to prayer will settle down upon you at every step you take, even to your dying day."[1]

Live a "life of prayer," and you'll see and experience many wonderful answers to it while you live on this earth. Of course, God's answer to prayer isn't always the one we hoped for and expected, but it is always for our ultimate good. The important thing is to saturate your day with prayer and then to be alert to God's workings in the world around you: the neighbor you reached out to comes to Christ, your troubled teenager turns to God and away from a life of drugs, the church you've served grows in size and ministry, the nation you covered in prayer prospers, the husband for whom you've labored in prayer for years finally advances in spiritual growth, the children you've taught in Sunday school grow into joyful adolescents and teenagers aware of God's unconditional love for them.

But here's the really exciting part: the gentle rain of answered prayers won't stop just because your address changes to heaven. Even when you've passed out of this world into eternity, your loved ones will step under the showers of your prayers' blessings. The impact will continue for years, even for generations.

Understanding this truth can truly revolutionize your spiritual life: *your prayers will outlive your life.*

It's true! When you send your prayers heavenward, God hears and receives them. And the fact is, our petitions may not be answered today or next week or next year, but that doesn't mean they don't have an impact. Revelation 5:8 speaks of the "golden bowls full of incense . . . , which are the prayers of God's people" (AMP). Our prayers are set before God, and they don't go away when our physical bodies die. They don't disappear when the mouth that cried out to God is silenced. God doesn't get busy doing other things just because we stop uttering these petitions in our daily time with him. Our prayers are always before him. Even when we see him face to face and as we enjoy the glories of heaven in his presence, our prayers will go on being answered in the lives of people we interceded for.

As E. M. Bounds said, "The prayers live on before God and God's heart is set on them and prayers outlive the lives of those who uttered them, they outlive a generation, outlive an age, outlive a world."[2]

One of the best examples of this truth is the story of a little boy named John who grew up in London many years ago. His mother, Elizabeth, taught him the catechism, took him to church, and read the Bible to him every day. She prayed earnestly for her son, and as she did, she was led to pray that he would become a pastor someday. However, when she told her husband, an English ship captain, about her prayers, he adamantly insisted that John would never be anything but a ship captain who earned his living on the seas, as he did.

For a while, it seemed John's father was right. Before he was seven years old, John's young mother died of tuberculosis. His father remarried and set off on yet another sea voyage, shuttling the boy away to live with an uncaring stepmother in the country. The spiritual influence in his life seemed to be lost. When he was eleven years old, he was put on a ship for his first voyage, and his training for the vocation of ship captain began.

John's life spiraled downward into moral darkness and depravity in the twenty-two years that followed. He became one of the most wicked, blasphemous slave traders in England, and he escaped death numerous times. Yet one night in a terrible storm at sea, he cried out to God and found himself remembering prayers from his childhood—his mother's loving words and the truths of the Bible she had shared with him. In that moment, he reached out to God's outstretched arms and was saved by a miraculous display of grace. He commemorated his salvation by writing what has become one of the best-known and beloved hymns of all times: "Amazing grace, how sweet the sound, that saved a wretch like me. I once was lost, but now am found, was blind but now I see."

Although the first part of his life was a ruin and a disgrace, John Newton came back to England after his dramatic conversion at sea, and against many odds, he trained to become a pastor and served God for *forty-four years*—twice as long as he had run from him. He wrote hundreds of hymns and was instrumental in influencing William Wilberforce and the British Parliament to stop the slave trade in England and its colonies forever.

Through his hymn "Amazing Grace," millions of people have been drawn closer to God. His mother's prayers had not only blessed her own son's life and "prevailed in spite of all Satan's efforts to destroy her son and keep him from becoming God's instrument"[3] but also impacted generations of people after her own life and her son's ministry had ended.

Just as Elizabeth Newton's prayers outlived her life, so will those you pray for schools and colleges, companies you worked for, and co-workers. Your prayers will not only have an influence on this present generation and world but will impact generations to come until Christ returns. That's why it's so important to continue praying and not give up. Even when one's life is over, God is faithful to answer his or her prayers.

George Mueller's life is a testimony to God's faithfulness. Besides praying for and supporting four thousand orphaned boys and girls through faith and prayer alone, rather than fund-raising efforts, Mueller had a particular burden for five close friends who didn't know God.

He prayed daily for five years until his first friend committed his life to Christ. The second friend must have been a bit more resistant— Mueller prayed for him *ten years* before he surrendered to God. The next two conversions took more than *twenty-five years of prayer*, but Mueller never gave up, and at last those two friends came into the fold. To his chagrin, at the end of his life, one of his friends hadn't yet turned to God. But after fifty-two years of prayer, at George Mueller's funeral service, that man gave his life to Christ.[4] None of these people could outrun the prayers of their persevering friend and intercessor.

Sometimes children put feet to their mother's prayers, continuing the legacy with action in a way she never could have dreamed. Robin Brown, a Connecticut woman, has carried a prayer assignment for the Yanomami Indians of northern Brazil for almost forty years. As a teenager she heard the gospel and gave her life to Christ. At one of the first teen meetings she attended, she heard a Bible translator named Don talk about how he was about to leave for pioneer missionary work in the Amazon rain forest of Brazil. He would learn the language so it could be written down, then he planned to translate the New Testament into their language, a very difficult task that would take years and years.

From the beginning, Robin was a prayer partner in Don's

ministry. She married, and eventually she and her husband had three sons, yet through it all she continued to stay in touch with Don. Her sons grew up praying for individual Yanomami tribes people and for Don's ministry, and later her kids were pen pals with Don's kids. Several decades later, all three of Robin's sons married, and now they and their wives have embraced the rugged life of being missionaries among these animistic Amazon people, living a hundred miles from the nearest civilized town. Their family has been praying and "plowing" the ground of northern Brazil for forty years. One thing they know: more prayer is necessary for this spiritual battle to see a breakthrough—but they are confident as they, their sons, wives, and grandchildren persevere in prayer and ministry, that God, who is the Author and Finisher of their faith, will also complete his good work among the Yanomami tribes.

THE LEGACY OF PRAYER

Some people have the resources to leave a large sum of money to their loved ones when they die. Others will leave a great legacy that results in hospital and university buildings being named after them. A few will leave vast real estate holdings or thriving family businesses. But the greatest legacy we can leave to those who come after us is the legacy of prayer. You can give your children, your nieces and nephews, and your loved ones and friends many gifts in this life and be a positive influence. But there is no greater gift you can give them than your prayers.

Back in the late 1600s in England, there were no washing

machines, dishwashers, or microwave ovens, of course. Everything had to be washed by hand and cooked from scratch. Wood had to be gathered and fires made so the family didn't freeze, and all this work was usually the woman's responsibility. These were busy women indeed!

One particular woman had an especially difficult life. Besides suffering a lingering sickness, she was married to a difficult, undependable, and at times tyrannical man. He was absent for long periods, and she was left with the entire load of child-rearing and household duties. Their family home burned, not once but twice, and almost everything they owned was destroyed. The woman faced mounting financial problems because of her husband's debts—and because she had nine children to raise. (She bore nineteen, but only nine lived into adulthood.)

This woman had a Martha schedule, to be sure, but she also had a Mary heart. She had grown up in a home where her parents wove prayer throughout her family's everyday life. She took this practice into her own home. Each day before she taught her children their lessons, she set aside an hour for reading the Bible and praying with them.

After her ninth child was born, she decided that one hour for prayer wasn't enough, and she made it two—adding the time from six to seven in the evening. At times she was known to pull her long skirt over her head for privacy while she talked to the Lord. She faced crushing difficulties and endless tasks, yet those who knew her attributed her spiritual legacy of courage and peace to the time she spent with God each day.

Although she was devoted to training her children, teaching them six hours every day, she knew their spiritual maturity would actually come from divine help. Her own efforts would not be enough. This passion for the souls of her children and their spiritual growth consumed her. Her biography describes how she would tuck her children in bed each night and lift her candle to gaze upon each face. As she did so, she prayed that God would enable her to so inspire her children that they could be used by him to change the world.

Susanna Wesley's prayers impacted not only her own and her children's generation but they outlived her life and touched future generations as well. Her son John became a powerful preacher whose sermons brought awakening, both in England and the colonies; he founded the Methodist movement, which culminated in the organization of the Methodist Church that still impacts the world today. Her son Charles wrote hundreds of hymns in addition to bringing the gospel to countless people.

When we pray, we are building a legacy of faith that will bless generations of people during our lifetime and beyond, not only in our own family but even around the world. The prayer life of a man named George McCluskey demonstrates that truth.

When George McCluskey married and started a family, he decided to invest one hour a day in prayer because he wanted his children to follow Christ. Every morning between eleven and noon, he prayed for the next *three* generations: his children, grandchildren, and great-grandchildren.

The years went by, and his two daughters committed their lives to

Christ and married men who went into full-time ministry. The two couples produced four girls and one boy. Each of those four girls married a minister, and the boy became a pastor.

The first two children born to the next generation were both boys. Upon graduation from high school, the two cousins chose the same college and became roommates. During their sophomore year, one of the boys decided to go into the ministry. The other didn't. He undoubtedly felt some pressure to continue the family legacy, but he chose instead to pursue his interest in psychology.

He earned his doctorate and eventually wrote books for parents that became bestsellers. He started a radio program that now is heard by millions of listeners each day. The man's name—James Dobson.[5]

Through the legacy of faith passed down from a great-grandfather he never met, Dr. Dobson and the ministries of Focus on the Family have brought salvation, practical help, and enduring hope to millions of families in America and more than 170 countries throughout the world. In addition, the *Focus on the Family* radio program is broadcast by six thousand stations worldwide. Dobson and his wife, Shirley, have led the National Day of Prayer, and he has influenced government leaders. These ministries shine around the world, focusing on God's light and love, and they all began with the persistent prayers of a man who prayed.

When I have spoken at churches that are alive and making an impact—churches that are bringing people to Christ, reaching out to the poor and the lost in their cities, and expanding Christ's kingdom abroad through missions—I've asked where their energy and power come from. Over and over I've been told things like, "Oh, it was the prayers of a group of older ladies who prayed for this church for fifty (or sixty or more) years. The few who haven't died are still praying today."

Think of it. Ponder this wonderful truth: *your prayers will outlive your life!* They will have the greatest influence of anything you can do to change the world or better the lives of those you love. More impact for good can be wrought through praying for others than through your physical work or your material success or any amount of money you could leave as an inheritance. It will matter more than all the talking or teaching you could ever do. It is the most powerful force in the world because God hears, answers, and never forgets our prayers.

Praying through Your Busy Day

Realizing the power your prayers can have, not only for your current situation, but for generations to come, can give a fresh new sense of purpose and a boost of energy to your prayer life. Here are some ideas for empowering your prayers—and you—for the long haul.

Pray for the People You Want to See in Heaven

One of Satan's biggest lies tells you that your prayers don't matter and that it's a waste of time to pray. A mother very concerned for her three rebellious teenage boys recently asked me, "Do you mean that praying for my sons really could make a difference? I've been so discouraged because my prayers haven't done much in the last few months to change the boys' lives, and it seemed pointless to continue. That makes it easy for me to neglect prayer."

Be assured, those aren't God's thoughts! Your prayers *do* matter—not just now, but for generations to come. That's why Satan tries to discourage you and distract you, because he knows how powerful and wide-reaching prayer is. When you worry, Satan doesn't work. But when you're on your knees, he worries!

You may need to persevere longer than the few months this mother of teens had been praying, longer than you'd planned on praying until the answer comes, but as E. M. Bounds said, "Prayer is mighty in its operations, and God never disappoints those who put their trust and confidence in him. They may have to wait long for the answer, and they may not live to see it, but the prayer of faith never misses its object."[6]

In fact, Dick Eastman, founder of Every Home for Christ and Change the World School of Prayer, has said that intercessory prayer is involved in *every person* who comes to a knowledge and relationship with Jesus Christ.[7] "We are born-again believers because other intercessors, some not even known to us, have touched our lives over the years, breaking the demonic darkness about us that might otherwise have kept us from a full knowledge of Christ,"[8] he said.

Eastman himself became a Christian because his mother faithfully prayed for him when he was a rowdy teenager who was stealing for sport, and her prayers turned his life around. Long after her death, he became one of the leaders of the prayer movement and taught thousands of people around the world how to impact their world with prayer. He has mobilized the church as a prayer force for the Great Commission in the United States and many countries abroad.

Make a VIP list of people you want to have eternal life, just as George Mueller did for his five friends. Regularly, even daily, bring them to God in prayer, and the Lord will link up his power in answer to your prayers, no matter how long it takes.

Ask for the Spirit of Prayer

Have you ever felt your prayers were as stale as leftover bread and weren't accomplishing anything? Have you been frustrated that your petitions haven't been answered yet? Or maybe you found yourself thinking, as you read this chapter, *I don't know if my puny prayers can impact anybody, least of all those generations yet to come.* Or perhaps you feel intimidated when you think of spiritual giants like Susanna Wesley. If you're encountering any of these or other obstacles, or if you're just struggling along praying without inspiration or conviction that God is really able to handle things, ask him simply and honestly for the Spirit of prayer.

O. Hallesby advised, "Pray a little each day in a childlike way for the Spirit of prayer. If you feel that you know, as yet, very little concerning the deep things of prayer and what prayer really is, then pray for the Spirit of prayer. There is nothing he would rather do than unveil to you the grace of prayer."[9]

Ask God to reveal to you the longevity of prayer, how the prayers of others have impacted you, and how your prayers can influence generations to come. It can be the beginning of a whole new start in your relationship with him.

QUESTIONS FOR DISCUSSION OR JOURNALING

1. Who do you know today who is a primary intercessor for you? Or who may have come before you as your intercessor, leaving you a legacy of prayer—a great-grandmother, your mother or aunt, a teacher, or a friend? Take a few minutes to thank God for these intercessors by name, and if they are still alive, find a way to thank them either in person or in a written note.

2. To whom do you want to leave a legacy of prayer and faith?

3. Read about the prayers of Epaphras in Colossians 4:12, which says he prayed "earnestly." (The New International Version translates it as, "He is always wrestling in prayer.") The saints before us understood the truth this verse expresses—prayer is work, but it's the most important work of all and worthy of our effort, time, and passion. What do you consider your most important work? What does your use of time say about your priorities?

4. What concern for the future do you have that you could turn into prayer? For your children or grandchildren to marry godly spouses? That the Great Commission will be taken to all the unreached groups and nations around the globe? For your family's future in an uncertain world?

PART TWO

Overcoming the Barriers

6

Praying with a Godward Focus

Faith focuses your eyes on God and his promises,
faithfulness, and availability.
Faith sees God present, deeply concerned, and active.
Faith looks at the problems and needs from God's perspective.
—Wesley Duewel

In August 2004, the orders were suddenly changed for the First Regiment, Third Marine Battalion (known as the 1/3), based in Hawaii. Because of the escalating violence in the Middle East, instead of embarking from Okinawa to a scheduled seven-month Pacific deployment, they were sent to the Persian Gulf to engage in combat in the Iraq War—beginning with the battle of Fallujah.

As coalition forces geared up for the major assault, the battalion surgeon and the sixty medics he led were warned to prepare for massive casualties. Fallujah erupted into a scene of continual violence, death, and destruction, and the battalion surgeon went to work each day after strapping on sixty pounds of body armor, ammunition, and medical supplies.

In his cargo pocket he carried two letters to be sent to his wife and daughter in case he didn't survive.

With bullets whizzing through the air and the concussion of aerial bombs and deadly rockets shaking the ground beneath them, the physician and the medics went into the front lines of heavy urban combat to care for the injured. The physician's job was to treat wounded marines and either send them to facilities in a safe zone for further medical care . . . or send them back into battle.

This military doctor I'm describing isn't just any sailor.

He is my son.[1]

A young man I love with all my heart, the child I carried for nine months, gave birth to (an event I vividly remember since he weighed nine pounds, twelve ounces!), raised through childhood, and cheered for as he walked across the stage to graduate from elementary school, high school, college, officer candidate school, and medical school.

My son.

In the war zone, he was a world away from the family and home he'd grown up in yet never far from my thoughts. In the beginning of his time in Iraq, I focused on the dangers Chris faced. I went to bed whispering prayers for him, found myself waking up in the night to pray for him, and prayed for him everywhere I went—driving, walking, working. My mind was absorbed with the enormity of the conflict and the huge dangers Chris and his men faced every day: improvised explosive devices (IEDs) and roadside bombs, rocket-propelled grenades (RPGs), random snipers' bullets, and suicide bombers.

"What is he doing there, Lord?" I asked one morning. "His battalion was supposed to be in the Pacific. They were supposed to be home in mid-January, and now their deployment has been extended . . ."

Then, in the quiet moment that followed, the Lord seemed to say to me, *Have you ever considered that Chris may very well be the answer to the prayers of other mothers who are praying that their sons and daughters will come home safely from the war?*

This thought truly inspired me because I felt great concern for the troops in Iraq and especially for those in Chris's battalion; I was honored that God might be using my son to answer another mother's prayer—and I too was praying for our soldiers.

But the reality of the situation—that Chris was probably being shot at by insurgents—was still very anxiety-producing.

In the first days of the battle, articles appeared in American newspapers about servicemen and women who had been wounded or killed in action. Then, to my eyes, the headlines became more personal: "1/3 Marines Vehicle Blown Up by Suicide Bomber" and "U.S. Soldiers Hit by Rare, Deadly Pneumonia." Since our son and his men were sleeping outdoors in seventeen-degree cold and he was caring for those with contagious diseases, that gave me something else to worry about in addition to the terrorists. When CNN flashed news across the screen that convoys in Chris's area were being targeted by insurgent attacks, my stomach tightened, my heart raced, and my anxiety rose.

Then, finally, I turned my focus Godward and tuned in to what he was saying.

Body Armor . . . and Spiritual Armor

I had prayed specific verses from the Bible for Chris before, but now the Spirit emphasized the importance of strategically dressing him in God's Word day by day. In the digital photo we received via e-mail, I could see the heavy body armor the military provided him, but I sensed the Lord saying Chris also needed the spiritual armor that prayer provided. As we rallied a contingency of family members, friends, and churches around the country to pray for Chris and the 1/3 Marines, I sensed right away that there would be so many verses I would need to record them in a special notebook.

I discovered that the more I prayed with a Godward focus and the more I incorporated Scripture verses into my prayers, the more I could pray in confidence instead of fear. I clung to the truth that God knew where my son was at every moment (even though on some weeks we didn't know his whereabouts) and that the Lord both goes before him and after him and is very much *with him.*

For instance, shaping my prayer around Psalm 139:1–10, I sometimes prayed, "Father, you know when Chris sits down and when he stands up. You know his every thought even when he's far away from home. You chart the path ahead of him . . . *Every moment you know where he is.* You both precede and follow him. You place your hand of blessing on his head . . . He can never escape from your Spirit! He can never get away from your presence (not even in the darkness and destruction in Iraq). Thank you, Lord, for keeping Chris—and me—in your heart and in your thoughts. Amen."

On Monday nights I joined my prayers for Chris and our armed forces with those of Ruthie, Cecilia, Lucy, and Jeanne—the other mothers in our military support group—and from them I gained much encouragement and inspiration. Their faith and prayers were a tremendous comfort and redefined the meaning and value of the term *support group* for me.

When I'd get preoccupied with the dangers and uncertainties surrounding Chris, God would send reminders. For instance, one day when my friend Anne and I were having lunch, I was expressing my concerns about Chris being in Iraq. "You know, Cheri," Anne said gently, "Chris is in God's hands, and all the days ordained for him were written in God's book before he was ever born."

God said it in Psalm 139:16, a verse that had been written on my heart years before. I just needed to be reminded of it and hear it again: "You saw me before I was born. Every day of my life was recorded in your book. Every moment was laid out before a single day had passed."

I'm not saying I didn't have stressful moments during Chris's deployment. There were plenty of situations that would push any military mom's panic button—like the day a Marine helicopter crashed in western Iraq and all thirty-one men aboard died, including a Lieutenant Fuller. For several hours we didn't know if our Lieutenant Fuller was safe or dead. But truths like those from Psalm 121 brought peace and hope to my heart. They reminded me that the One who created Chris also made the heavens and the earth and that he never tires or sleeps (see v. 3).

I knew God stood beside Chris in Iraq, keeping him from all evil and holding him close to his heart. Praying mothers have the hope and comfort of knowing their sons and daughters are in God's care and will be with God—either here or in heaven. And even as I felt relief when we finally learned that our Lieutenant Fuller was safe, I grieved for that other mother out there whose son had died, believing that she, too, was praying for her son.

Often I awoke in the middle of the night with the promise of Lamentations 3:23 front and center in my thoughts: "Great is his faithfulness; his mercies begin afresh each day." So I prayed, "Father, may your mercies be new for Chris when he wakes up today. Let him experience your mercy and dispense compassion in whatever the day holds for him."

When we received our son's Christmas letter, it ended with, "Please pray for Mercy (my radio call sign) and Peace (we all need it)." How kind of God that he had directed me to pray for many weeks specifically what Chris was asking for—*mercy*, the word he'd chosen as his call sign in combat.

Praying the Soldier's Psalm

As I continued to pray with a Godward focus, many Scripture passages comforted me, but the passage that was most highlighted for me was Psalm 91, the passage that had inspired my friend Cecilia to picture her son Jake in his machine-gun vehicle surrounded by powerful wings. In one month, "On Eagles' Wings," a song based on Psalm 91, seemed to be part of every conference or retreat I spoke at.

At one event I shared the podium with a petite, five-foot-four woman named Tracey who had served in the first phase of the Iraq War as a chaplain's bodyguard and had taken thousands of Psalm 91 stickers into Iraq right before the fighting started.

Tracey told how she had seen the Psalm 91 stickers over the beds of the wounded in Camp Viper, Iraq, how she had heard stories from soldiers of how the psalm had reassured them of God's presence in the midst of combat, and how they were praying this psalm, called "The Soldier's Psalm," for their own lives. The name comes from a World War I story about the Ninety-first Brigade of the U.S. Army, which prayed Psalm 91 together every day, led by their commander. Although they were engaged in several of the bloodiest battles in the war, these soldiers had no combat-related casualties—not because the passage was a good luck charm or a mantra, but because God's Word has power.

I didn't need any more convincing. I got some Psalm 91 stickers and put them in my Bible and other places to remind me to pray its words daily for Chris. I gave away stickers on the Marine base in Hawaii and around the country wherever I spoke, encouraging other military families to pray this psalm for their loved ones:

Those who live in the shelter of the Most High
will find rest in the shadow of the Almighty.

a busy woman's guide to prayer

This I declare of the LORD:
He alone is my refuge, my place of safety;
he is my God, and I am trusting him.

For he will rescue you from every trap
and protect you from the fatal plague.

He will shield you with his wings.
He will shelter you with his feathers.
His faithful promises are your armor and protection.

Do not be afraid of the terrors of the night,
nor fear the dangers of the day,
nor dread the plague that stalks in darkness,
nor the disaster that strikes at midday.

Though a thousand fall at your side,
though ten thousand are dying around you,
these evils will not touch you.

But you will see it with your eyes;
you will see how the wicked are punished.

If you make the LORD your refuge,
if you make the Most High your shelter,
no evil will conquer you;
no plague will come near your dwelling.

For he orders his angels
to protect you wherever you go.

They will hold you with their hands
to keep you from striking your foot on a stone.

You will trample down lions and poisonous snakes;
you will crush fierce lions and serpents under your feet!

The LORD says, "I will rescue those who love me.
I will protect those who trust in my name.

When they call on me, I will answer;
I will be with them in trouble.
I will rescue them and honor them.

I will satisfy them with a long life
and give them my salvation."

I found out later that a number of other people, on their own, had felt God moving them to pray Psalm 91 for our son. Throughout the months of Chris's deployment, the psalm's comforting words helped me move my focus away from the dangers Chris faced and onto God and his promises of protection in difficult times. With the psalm as my basis, I often prayed words like these:

"Lord, may my son and all our troops turn to you and find rest in the shadow of your wings. Keep Chris safe from all hidden dangers and all deadly diseases. Shield and shelter him with your wings, and let your faithful promises be his armor and protection. May he not be afraid of the terrors of the night or fear the dangers of the day or the disaster that strikes at midday. . . . As he makes you, the Lord, his refuge and shelter, let no evil conquer him, no plague come near his tent or dwelling. Please order your angels to protect him wherever he goes.

"Lord, you say, 'I will rescue those who love me. I will protect those who trust in my name.' May this be true for every man and woman in the 1/3 and for all our forces. When they call on you, Father, answer them, be with them in trouble, rescue them and honor them. Satisfy them with a long life and give them your salvation. Amen."

Answers came in interesting ways. One evening while I was visiting with my dear friend Patty and giving her an update on Chris's unit, she said, "Let's pray for Chris." She told me later that in the midst of our prayers, she saw clearly in her spirit a huge, camouflage-uniformed angel guarding Chris wherever he went. And although Chris treated many Marines who had contagious viruses and bacterial infections, he was never so sick himself that he couldn't get up and do his job.

Our son returned home to his wife, Maggie, and daughter, Josephine, in April 2005. And even as we were overjoyed and thankful for his safe return, we grieved for families whose loved ones didn't return and realize that it's no fairer that Chris lived than that others died. As I continue to pray for all our military troops serving around the world to come home safely to their families, our military moms group has built a Web site with scriptural prayers and encouragement for families whose loved ones are deployed. Please share it with any military families you know: www.militaryfamiliespray.com.

Your son, daughter, husband, or friend may not be in a literal combat zone, but everyone goes through spiritual warfare or attacks in one way or another—husbands struggle with pornography or depression, teens experience temptations to abuse drugs or alcohol. As my friend Jill Boyce said, although Psalm 91 is called the Soldier's Psalm, it's really for all of us. There is never a time our loved ones don't need our prayers in the battles of life.

FIXING OUR EYES ON THE LORD

I've learned firsthand that it's an altogether different experience to pray with a Godward focus—fixing my eyes on the Lord and the power of his Spirit—than it is to pray with my focus riveted tenaciously on my problems. When all I see is my problems, they soon loom so large I start wondering if praying will help. And few of us busy women are going to invest time in praying about something we think is too big or too hard for God to handle. When that's our mind-set, we start putting our energies into trying to fix the problems ourselves instead of handing over our problems to God so we can focus on Godward prayer.

When big waves of trials threaten to swamp us or overwhelm someone we love, it's easy to panic. If, in our distress, we focus on the current complications or on our own inability to control the situation (which, of course, we actually can't do because control is an illusion), then it's only a short, downward spiral into discouragement or prayer-lessness.

Focusing on God makes all the difference in how we pray. Martha Thatcher compared this process to what happens when she uses the focusing ring of her camera to choose what image will be central to her photograph. "It didn't take me long to realize that if I draw one image into focus, I automatically put several others out of focus," she said. "Although there are ways to increase the focusing range, I rather like having a good part of the picture slightly fuzzy. It encourages singular attention. The crisp central focus leaves no doubt about what is important to me in the picture. The result is perspective."[2]

When we zoom in and get the Lord in focus, our perspective changes. This is so important when we go through difficulties. The late Corrie ten Boom, in her marvelous little book *Reflections of God's Glory*, spoke of the need we all have for a renewed vision and a Godward focus. "Even John, the disciple whom Jesus loved, had to have his eyes on his eternal Lord," Corrie wrote. "We are not ready for the battle until we have seen the Lord, for Jesus is the answer to all problems."[3]

WHERE IS YOUR FOCUS?

When you get in a hard place, do you believe God is able? Are your thoughts riveted on the mountains of problems or on the Mountain-Mover? Have you experienced his faithfulness in the past so you know you can trust him in the future? Amazingly, even people who have been delivered in miraculous ways often forget God's power and develop what Oswald Chambers called a "grasshopper attitude" about the One who said he would never fail or forsake us. Then "the difficulties become like giants, we become like grasshoppers, and God becomes a nonentity."[4]

Gladys Alyward was called "Small Woman," but she had more courage than several men put together. She served in China for many years, and hundreds of Chinese people came to know Christ because of her ministry. Once she single-handedly stopped a prison riot in her village of YangCheng and brought peace and reform to the prison. But in World War II, the Japanese invaded China, and village by village, they attacked and slaughtered the people of YangCheng. Gladys was left with one hundred orphans to try to get to safety in free China. She had led the children hundreds of miles across mountain ranges and through terrible trials, but then they came to the Yellow River and had no way to get across.

In the most despairing night of her life, she heard the gunfire of the Japanese army approaching in the distance and was at the end of her strength and hope. Then a little girl reminded her of their beloved Moses and how God had parted the Red Sea for his people to escape from the Egyptians. That same God could rescue Small Woman and the children too, she said.

"But I am not Moses!" Gladys said.

"Yes, but Jehovah is still God!" the little girl, Sualan, exclaimed.

With those words, Gladys's attitude changed from a grasshopper to a Godward focus, and she believed that God had the ability to do the impossible. Filled with hope, she led the children in singing hymns to praise him. Nearby, a Chinese nationalist soldier heard a strange sound he thought was a helicopter and went across the river to investigate. When he saw the plight of the children and Small Woman, he made several trips back and forth to bring all of them across the river. They still had many miles to travel on foot to arrive at the orphanage in free China, but Gladys got the children there safely, eventually recovered from her wounds and sickness, and after the war, served in China the rest of her life.

Just as he did in Gladys Alyward's desperate circumstances, and just as he did in numerous situations throughout biblical history, the Lord encourages us in our problems and challenges us to trade in our grasshopper attitude about prayer for a Godward mentality. He calls us to lift our eyes away from whatever problems or difficulties we face and focus instead on the Lord and his faithfulness. As I heard Matt Massey, a Cincinnati pastor, say recently, "God is the Unstoppable Force. He is still doing great things in spite of the bad things going on in our world."

PRAYING WITH PRAISE

Be encouraged. God does not panic. He has great and mighty plans, and those plans will not be thwarted. Believe this, and you can look at your problems from above, from his perspective, instead of from beneath your mountains of difficulties. We must make this choice daily. It is a decision of the will, and I've found that one of the greatest helps in making it is *praise*.

We sing praise songs at the beginning of our church services, and many of us include praise and adoration as the first step in our ACTS prayer format (**a**doration, **c**onfession, **t**hanksgiving, and **s**upplication). Praise music is a wonderful gift, and a structure for prayer can be very helpful. But the praise I'm talking about here is more than either of those things. It's verbalizing aloud and setting our thoughts on who God is.

It's fine to first pour out our hearts and emotions to the Lord—after all, David, the man after God's own heart, cast his burdens and poured out his heart repeatedly in the Old Testament Psalms. He complained, he cried, and he emoted; he expressed fear, loneliness, sadness, and hurt. Similarly, we are encouraged to pour out our hearts and burdens as well, because God is our refuge just as he was David's (see Psalm 62:8).

But David always turned from his problems to acknowledge and declare God's greatness and attributes. We see this again and again in the psalms. For a good example, let's look at Psalm 13:

How long, O LORD? Will You forget me forever?
How long will You hide Your face from me?
How long shall I take counsel in my soul,
Having sorrow in my heart all the day?
How long will my enemy be exalted over me?
Consider and answer me, O LORD my God;
Enlighten my eyes, or I will sleep the sleep of death,
And my enemy will say, "I have overcome him,"
And my adversaries will rejoice when I am shaken.
But I have trusted in Your lovingkindness;
My heart shall rejoice in Your salvation.
I will sing to the LORD,
Because He has dealt bountifully with me. (NASB)

As the psalm begins, David's enemies are once again bearing down upon him to the point that he's afraid his death is imminent. The heavens seem like brass (ever been there?). He feels abandoned, as though God has forgotten about him, and he cries out in what sounds like abject misery: "Lord, where are you?"

But then his focus turns from the overwhelming problems to God—and he praises him, declaring what is true about God: his "lovingkindness," his gift of salvation, his bountiful support. Notice that David's words of worship came even before the problems were solved.

Prayers proclaiming God's character, his goodness and kindness, never fail to transform our focus and help us trust. We can simply say, "Lord, this is hard. But in the midst of it, you are good. You are faithful," or "Father, I don't know what we're going to do, but you promised to lead us, so I am trusting you." We don't have to use our own imaginations to think of words that lift up who God is. We have as our resource the whole Bible, where God reveals himself on page after page.

Each week in our College and Career Moms In Touch group,[5] we've found that praying God's attributes helps us remember who we are praying to before we ever make our petitions—and also that he is well able to deal with our greatest concerns.

Last week, we focused on God as our Guide, and as we began our prayer time, we went around the circle, reading aloud verses that helped us see him in that role. Some of the verses we read (all from NASB) were:

For such is God, our God forever and ever; He will guide us until death. (Psalm 48:14)

Your ears will hear a word behind you, "This is the way, walk in it," whenever you turn to the right or to the left. (Isaiah 30:21) I will instruct you and teach you in the way which you should go; I will counsel you with My eye upon you. (Psalm 32:8)

I will lead the blind by a way they do not know, in paths they do not know I will guide them. I will make darkness into light before them and rugged places into plains. (Isaiah 42:16)

As we shared with each other during the meeting, these verses reminded us that God is so gracious and merciful that he even serves as Guide for our sons and daughters who may not be consciously looking for his direction. Three women that day were burdened about the choices their children were facing: one who had five interviews for a job change, another who was changing colleges, and one son who was choosing a graduate school to attend. As we praised God as our Guide, these mothers were tremendously reassured that God is and will be their young adults' Guide through the covenant of the Lord Jesus, even when they aren't looking to him every moment for guidance. They were led to relinquish them and entrust them to their Guide instead of trying to interfere with the decision process themselves.

When we pray to God according to how he reveals himself in his Word, we can praise him and ask for his help with so much more confidence and hope. When I pray for a friend who is grieving her husband's death, I say, "This is who you are, Lord: you are the Comforter; you comfort those who mourn" (see Isaiah 61:1–3, Matthew 5:4). When I am praying about financial worries, I can say, "You are *Jehovahjireh,* the Lord our provider, so we can pray for this financial need, trusting that you will provide in your gracious way and timing" (see Luke 12:29–32).

When I pray for someone who is suffering physically or emotionally (and sometimes this person is *me*), I say, "Lord Jesus, you are close to those crushed in spirit; you heal the brokenhearted. You took our infirmities, sins, and sorrows on your own body on the cross. Please pour out your love and healing into their—or my—broken heart" (see Psalm 34:18 and Matthew 8:17).

When we pray God's attributes, we are asking right in line with who he is. Praying with this kind of Godward focus isn't just hoping the Lord will do something. It isn't just hoping that he might hear us. Prayer that centers on the sufficiency, the power, and the love of Christ is expectant and full of faith—not faith in our saying the right words, but in God's power and his awesome ability and desire to bless his children.

PRAYING GOD'S WORD

As I was reminded when our son was in Iraq, another part of praying with a Godward focus means praying biblical prayers. When I talk with women, one of their frustrations with prayer is not knowing what to say to the Lord or how to pray for his best to take place. We've all been there at one time or another. "I don't know what to pray," said a Washington woman. "It sounds better to me when someone else prays," said another. "I'm a new believer, and I don't feel like my words are right. They aren't as eloquent as the prayers I hear other people say."

Praying God's Word will expand your prayer vocabulary and revive your spiritual life. Use the Bible as your prayer handbook. Without his Word, our prayers can become vague and unfocused or dry and lifeless, like plants we forget to water. With his Word, our prayers are nourished and energized, and what we need to pray is illumined.

Scripture tells us that God's Word is living and active, sharper than a two-edged sword (see Hebrews 4:12). And he promises that his Word will bear fruit, that it will not return to him empty, but will accomplish the purpose for which it was sent (see Isaiah 55:11). As we read his Word with this in mind, it will motivate us to pray.

When we pray biblical prayers, we are praying for the things that are on God's heart, which is a wonderful thing. "Praying is popularly viewed as requesting from God, and so it is," said Judson Cornwall. "But when we bring the Scriptures into our prayer, praying often becomes responding to God. Our prayer is a reaction to what we have just heard God say."[6] As we pray God's promises, our prayers become filled with faith instead of doubt. Rather than wringing our hands, we begin to trust him to fulfill his Word in his way and timing.

Praying through Your Busy Day

As we pray with a Godward focus we're more likely to pray in the will of God, for God always stands behind what he has said. Here are a couple of practical ideas that will help you keep your eyes on the One who is able.

Let the Bible Inspire Your Prayers

Think of a situation you're facing. When you read the Bible this week, ask God to highlight a verse or passage you can incorporate into your prayer concerns. Write it down, stick it in your Bible or on the dashboard of the car, and pray it back to him—not once but in a persevering, ongoing way until it's answered.

For example, if you are exhausted with too many things on your plate, you could pray Psalm 145:14–21: "Lord, you say that you lift the fallen and those bent beneath their loads. The eyes of everyone look up to you for help. You give them their food as they need it. I trust you to lift me up, help me bear this load, and sustain me" (adapted from TLB).

Or when you are doubting, pray, "Lord, when doubts fill my mind, when my heart is in turmoil, quiet me and give me renewed hope and cheer" (adapted from Psalm 94:19).

If you are disheartened by your situation, pray, "Lord, help me be satisfied with my present circumstances and with what I have, for you have said, 'I will not in any way fail you nor give you up, nor leave you without support. I will not, I will not, I will not in any degree leave you helpless, nor forsake nor let you down, nor relax My hold on you.' So I'll take comfort and be encouraged and confidently and boldly say, 'The Lord is my Helper; I will not be seized with alarm. I will not fear or dread or be terrified. What can man do to me?'" (adapted from Hebrews 13:5–6 AMP).

Pray God's Attributes

As we've discussed in this chapter, learning God's attributes and names can be a great boost to your prayer life. Psalm 9:10 says that those who know God's name and nature trust in him.

Don't just *learn* God's attributes, *use them* to praise him. As someone said, "Impossibilities and hopeless situations are an opportunity to glorify the Lord before the visible and invisible world, for nothing is so honoring to him as when we pray in faith and proclaim his greatness."[7] This kind of prayer is also an important part of spiritual warfare, and it fills us with faith.

In fact, the British pastor Charles Spurgeon and other classic Christians of history encouraged what they called "pleading God's attributes," as David did in Psalm 51:1: "Have mercy on me, O God, *according to your unfailing love; according to your great compassion* blot out my transgressions" (NIV).

Spurgeon said, "Faith will plead all the attributes of God—You are good, reveal Your bounty to Your servant; You are immutable—You have done this for others of your servants; do it for me."[8]

Look up these attributes or names of God[9] and choose one to incorporate into your prayer time this week:

Jehovahnissi, meaning "The Lord My Banner." "His banner over me is love" (see Exodus 17:15 and Song of Songs 2:4 KJV and NLT).

Jehovahjireh, meaning "The Lord Will Provide." He knows our needs and provides for them (see Genesis 22:14 KJV and NLT).

Jehovahshalom, meaning "The Lord Is Peace." He gives us inner peace (see Judges 6:24 KJV and NLT).

Jehovahraah, meaning "The Lord Is My Shepherd." He promises to lead and guide us, to speak to us, and show us what direction to go (see Psalm 23).

Jehovahrapha, meaning, "The Lord Who Heals" (see Exodus 15:25–27 NASB; Psalm 103:3, 147:3; 1 Peter 2:24).

If these Jehovah names sound too foreign for you to connect with, look up these characteristics of God's nature in the concordance of your Bible: Counselor, Comforter, Light of the World, Helper.

Questions for Discussion and Journaling

1. Which one of the names of God listed above connects most powerfully with a need you are currently experiencing?

2. Do you have a grasshopper attitude, or do you focus on God's power when you pray? What can you learn from Gladys Alyward's experience or from the story of Joshua and Caleb and the spies sent ahead to the Promised Land (see Numbers 13–14)?

3. When difficulties or storms hit your life, what do you tend to focus on? What's your first resource—the person, place, or thing you immediately turn to?

4. What does God's Word say in Isaiah 26:3 about the benefits of turning to and fixing your thoughts on the Lord? How would your life be different if you really believed and walked in the truth of Isaiah 26:3?

5. Faith looks at God instead of looking inward at inadequacies, problems, or circumstances. Is there an area of your life where you need to redirect your focus? What is it?

7

Connecting with God in a
Noisy, Fast-Paced World

Listening to the Lord is the first thing, the second thing,
and the third thing necessary for successful intercession.

—Richard Foster

It was one of those overly packed days in which tasks seemed to multiply and there weren't enough hours in the day to get them all done. I had taken care of my darling, energetic two-year-old grandson Luke all morning while his mom was out of town. Luke and I enjoy playing with little toy cowboys and Indians and reading books together. I'd fed him breakfast, done housework, and taken him and the dog for a walk. Then, after taking Luke out to lunch, we went to the grocery store, where we found a little toy rifle he was thrilled with. (By that time, I was reminded why God gave little children to much younger women than I!)

After dropping him at the babysitter's house, I headed for the office and typed like crazy for three hours to meet a magazine deadline, answer e-mail, and polish a speech for a weekend conference before making a stop at the post office to mail some book orders and a package to Chris in Iraq. It's exhausting even now, just revisiting that day!

Though I was tired, I drove over to the YMCA to walk on the treadmill because I knew it would be my last chance of the day to exercise. If I went home now, I'd crash and never make it back to the Y.

I hopped on the treadmill and started the belt. After a few minutes of walking, I realized the television sets hadn't been changed to the right channels for the afternoon—*again.* Somewhat annoyed because the channels were supposed to have been changed a few hours earlier and they were too high for me to reach, I got off the treadmill and went to the desk to ask the attendant to make the change.

Unfortunately, I was in such a hurry and so focused on getting those channels changed that I hadn't paid attention to something *very important*: the treadmill belt was still moving. I hadn't taken the time to turn it off. So when I got back on the machine, it threw me right off, and I fell, crashing onto the hard metal edge of the treadmill, bruising my knee, and smacking my left arm and elbow. In moments, fellow exercisers had gotten off their treadmills and elliptical trainers (and, being a lot smarter than I was, they had turned off their machines as they did so), and were staring down at me, asking, "Are you all right?"

Of course I *wasn't* all right. The exercise director hurried to my side with an ice pack and a towel to stop the bleeding.

By this time, you're probably thinking I am really crazy or careless. But the incident underscores the fact that accidents happen when you're rushed and not paying attention. (My defensive-driving instructor said those factors are among the leading causes of car wrecks.)

Despite more ice packs, Bactine, and Band-Aids, a few hours later my arm was swollen, bruised, and seeping blood. My friend Peggy drove me to the after-hours clinic at our local emergency room. (Luke was spending the night with his dad and his other grandmother.)

"This wound has to heal from the inside out," the doctor told me as he examined my elbow. (I think this is how God works with us too.) "And since tissue was ripped out of your skin when you fell, it can't be sutured. This may slow down your exercise for a few days," he said.

Ouch! *Surely I haven't prayed that dangerous prayer, "Slow me down, Lord,"* I thought as the ER doctor was carefully irrigating and bandaging my arm.

My mind went back to another mishap two months earlier that had resulted from my attempt to squeeze too many things into too short a time period. I came home from a power walk to a smoke-filled house and a note on my kitchen counter: "Mr. and Mrs. Fuller: I am Captain Hall with the Edmond Fire Department. You left a pan on the stove which started smoking and set off your alarm. We made entry into your home through an open window. We ventilated the smoke out and locked up when we left. Thank you." (Thank *me?* I thanked the firefighters and God for smoke alarms and a quick-moving fire department!)

I had hurriedly left the house without turning off the navy bean soup, and after walking, I had detoured by my daughter's house and the hair salon she runs out of her home. She was doing ten haircuts back to back, and I stayed to sweep the floor for her.

While I was gone, our dinner went up in smoke, and the house almost did too.

Thinking back on that episode the morning after the treadmill accident, I sat with my arm propped up and my Bible in my lap and thought, *Oh, Lord, I am such a slow learner. I know you want me to rest in you instead of rush, but I always seem to have too much to do. When am I going to stop this racing around?*

By no coincidence, my reading for that day was a passage in Psalm 39 that says, "LORD, remind me. . . . We are merely moving shadows, *and all our busy rushing ends in nothing*" (vv. 4, 6, emphasis mine).

Oh, how patient God is to speak to us . . . again and again. And now I was listening at last. It's just sad it took an expensive trip to the emergency room to get my attention.

Can you relate? Do you ever operate in overdrive? Do you ever start your day in peace and then get pushed into constant hurrying by unexpected demands that flood in and turn your schedule upside down? Fast-forward probably isn't the speed we would *choose* for getting through the day, but when the needs of family, work, and other responsibilities pile up, rushing seems to be the only way to cope. Or maybe we're being unrealistic about what we can get done in twenty-four hours.

According to physician Brent W. Bost, millions of women

struggle with what he calls "hurried woman syndrome," juggling work and motherhood, volunteer work, church and household activities, and other caretaking. Some of us are married. Some are not. But we are always running someplace. And what does all this busy rushing result in? Fatigue, depression, moodiness, weight gain, and chronic stress.[1]

I'm reminded again of that scene when Jesus visited two of his dearest friends. Martha was the one who seemed to be continually in a hurry, like many of us today, while Mary was content to sit at Jesus's feet and listen to him. Martha complained to him as she fussed and fumed over the big dinner she was preparing, "Lord, doesn't it seem unfair to you that my sister just sits here while I do all the work? Tell her to come and help me" (Luke 10:40).

"Martha, Martha, you are busy and distracted and so upset over all these details!" Jesus answered. "There is really only one thing worth being concerned about [some translations say 'one most necessary thing']. Mary has discovered it—and I won't take it away from her."[2] Instead of sending Mary to the kitchen, he commended her.

It wasn't that Jesus didn't appreciate Martha's efforts. Remember, he and his disciples returned to that home again and again to enjoy her hospitality. I don't think he was putting down the Marthas of biblical times or the Marthas of today. After all, they are productive, energetic women who are running businesses, supporting ministries and missionaries, planning and coordinating women's conferences, taking care of family and friends, feeding the hungry and the sick in their congregations, and often teaching the children, to boot.

But what was that one necessary and most important thing Mary did that pleased the Lord so?

She was earnestly listening to Jesus with her heart.

Is Anybody Listening?

God spoke the world into existence. "God said, 'Let there be light,' and there was light" (Genesis 1:3). By his words, he created everything in our universe. And you know, the Lord is still speaking today. Psalm 50:3 says God "shall not keep silence" (KJV). In Psalm 29, David says, "The God of glory thunders, the LORD is over many waters. The voice of the LORD is powerful, the voice of the LORD is majestic" (vv. 3–4 NASB). Psalm 32:8 says, "I will instruct you and teach you in the way which you should go" (NASB), and in Isaiah 30:21 we read, "Your ears shall hear a word behind you, saying, 'This is the way, walk in it'" (NKJV).

Whereas God spoke in both the Old Testament and the New Testament, listening to the Lord isn't just for Bible days. Jesus said his sheep would hear his voice (see John 10:27). Well, *we* are his sheep, and he invites us to listen and follow.

Sometimes he speaks in a whisper. As I discovered again in my treadmill incident, sometimes he speaks in our pain. And often he speaks in a way that is *contrary to our natural inclinations*, as E. Stanley Jones, a Methodist missionary, once discovered.

Jones was a great man of faith, prayer, and evangelism, but in order to raise enough money to keep the missions in India going, he took a marathon fund-raising journey for two weeks every year. He flew to one city and spoke to a group at breakfast, another at lunch, and a third group at dinner; then he flew off to another city to repeat his appeals to three more churches or organizations the next day . . . and the next.

One evening he raced to the airport to catch the last flight so he could get to his next day's speaking engagements. He had booked the ticket several months ahead, and as he waited at the gate for his seat assignment the airline representative suddenly announced that the flight was oversold. Would some passengers voluntarily give up their seats?

Jones thought he heard God's still small voice whisper to him, *Step out of the line.* But he tried to ignore the message. He knew if he didn't take this flight he would miss his meetings the following day, at least the first two of them. And the ministry needed the money he would raise from those engagements.

When he was almost at the ticket counter, he again sensed God urging him to give up his seat. But again he hesitated. However, when he was just one person away from the agent, he heard God speak, this time very clearly, *STEP OUT OF THE LINE!* That time Jones obeyed.

Tragically, that airplane crashed, and all crew members and passengers aboard were killed.

When news reporters heard that Dr. E. Stanley Jones had not been aboard as scheduled, they stood in line to interview him. After hearing why he hadn't been aboard the doomed flight, they were angry. "Do you mean to say that you were the only person God loved enough to warn?" they asked.

"Oh, no!" came his reply. "I know God loved every person aboard that plane at least as much as he loves me. But I was the only one who was listening."

Our God is still speaking to his people today.

The question is . . . *are we listening?*

The Challenge of Listening

For most of us women, listening isn't what we do best. The average woman spends approximately one-fifth of her life talking, and it all adds up to about thirty thousand words a day, enough in one year to fill sixty-six books—and not short books, either, but each one eight hundred pages long. Men, however, have only about ten thousand words to say each day. No wonder we get frustrated with our husbands' lack of communication! When they come home, they've already spoken most of their ten thousand words during the work day, and we're just getting started!

Listening is even more of a challenge with all the noise and information overload around us: televisions and CD players, cell phones going off with melodic or annoying rings, iPods, BlackBerries, and whatever clamor the latest technology offers. Sometimes, with all these distractions, we become more tuned in to the sounds in the world around us than to God's voice.

Hurried women aren't naturally good listeners. Consider, for example, the woman whose little boy came home from kindergarten wanting to tell her about something that happened on the playground. As she busily prepared lunch in the kitchen, the five-year-old followed her around while she chopped up chicken for the salad, threw a load of clothes in the dryer, and caught a little noon news on the kitchen-counter TV set. A friend was arriving for lunch soon, and she wanted to be ready. Yet her son continued telling his story in a way that only little kids can expound.

"Mommy, are you listening?" he asked several times.

"Sure, honey; I'm listening," she answered as her eyes drifted back to a breaking news story.

Again he tried to tell her what seemed to be important to him. Finally the child tugged on his mom's jeans until he pulled her down to his eye level.

"But, Mommy, would you listen with your face?"

I think God wants that from us as well; he wants us to listen to him with our face and our heart, to give him our full attention and focus. Because if we want to become the women God created us to be, if we want miracles and blessing in our lives and the lives of those we love, we need to learn to listen.

When we don't listen, we miss the very direction we need from God. Then prayer becomes a one-sided conversation. Think what it would be like if, every time you and your friend got together to talk, *the only one* who spoke was you—how much you'd miss of your friend's thoughts, ideas, and heart responses.

Or what if, when you went to the doctor, you sat down and told him your symptoms and then before he could advise you on medical treatment you ran out of the room? The doctor's appointment wouldn't yield much help.

When we do listen to God, it's amazing what can happen. Just a few words from him can transform our attitude and our life, provide us with a whole new direction, heal a relationship, or give hope to someone who is desperate for it.

If only we listen . . . and obey.

THE DOOR OF OBEDIENCE

Andrew Murray, the great nineteenth-century Dutch Reformed pastor, called obedience the path to power in prayer. "Obedience and faith are simply two parts of one act—surrender to God and his will. . . . Obedience is the only path that leads to the glory of God."[3]

There is an old saying that advises, When you're not hearing from God, think back to a place where you failed to obey him. Do what he instructed you to do back there at the bend of the road, and you'll find things will open up and you'll begin to hear his voice again. God "not only wants to lead us, but if we listen obediently and follow him, then we are at peace," said Corrie ten Boom.[4] And along the path of obedience, you may find some surprising blessings.

Beloved Christian author and speaker Catherine Marshall learned one of her greatest lessons of obedience from insomnia. Because she suffered from chronic sleeplessness, her doctor prescribed sleeping pills. After years of taking them, Catherine felt God questioning her dependence on the medication. But she ignored his persistent warnings, afraid he would ask her to do something she didn't want to do. Besides, she desperately needed sleep so she could get her writing done and meet the publisher's deadlines.

One day when she was boarding an airplane, she realized she'd left her bottle of sleeping pills at home. Thinking this was how God was going to give her a breakthrough with her insomnia, she asked him to let her sleep naturally. But that night, sleep wouldn't come. She tossed and turned all night—and came face to face with just how dependent she was on the pills.

On the way home she inquired, "Lord, am I hearing you right on this? Do you want me to stop using these foolish little pills?"

It was as if God was just waiting for her to ask. *Yes,* he whispered to her heart. *The pills are foolish. But the real issue is—you want sleep more than you want me. Lay your desire for sleep on the altar, Catherine. Give it to me. I have great blessings in store for you.*

Taking a courageous step and hoping for a miracle, Catherine threw all her sleeping pills away and informed God she was going to depend completely on him to get her rest. For eight days and nights, she couldn't sleep. When she did, she had terrifying dreams about rejection and danger. During the day she was exhausted and nervous; during the long nights, she was miserably awake.

"Lord, I obeyed you, and look what's happened! I'm worse off than before!" she wailed.

Again God gently assured her, *You want the instant miracle of sleep on demand. I'm interested in healing the whole person.*

Finally, on the eighth night, Catherine was able to sleep. Not only did she sleep soundly, she dreamed of God's steadfast love and care. He brought healing not only to her insomnia but also to the deep fears of rejection and danger she'd suffered all her life. Catherine's road to freedom, both from sleeping pills and inner turmoil, led through the door of obedience to God's quiet whisper.[5]

MY DWELLING PLACE

I have personally experienced the truth of how just hearing a few words from the Lord and yielding to him can change my heart. In one of those times, I was walking around the block that had been our neighborhood for the previous three years. We had bought our first house there, wallpapered the kitchen, painted the whole house, grown red roses in the garden, and built a wonderful fort for our boys in the backyard. It was home to our two young sons and the little girl we'd brought there when she was three weeks old. I had started a play-group with other moms who had become my close friends, and for the first time in our ten years of marriage, I felt truly at home.

That's why I dreaded the thought of our impending move. Everything pointed to the fact that the move was best. And I wanted to be obedient to God, like Bible heroes Sarah and her husband, Abraham. They said yes to God's call to travel to unknown places and live as strangers, camping in tents because they were keeping their eyes on an unseen city in the future that had eternal foundations— the home designed and built by God himself (see Hebrews 11:8–10). Well, maybe I didn't *really* want to live in a tent, but I did sense that God wanted me to be flexible instead of being stuck in my way.

I could have said, "No, Holmes, I just don't want to move," but I knew that would go against how the Lord was leading us. Yet I was struggling because I really loved this little home.

"Lord, you know I'm a nester by heart," I prayed. "I'd just love to remain where we are. I don't even need to move the furniture to be content, much less change houses. Staying right here would be just fine with me."

As I mentally wrestled with God about why we were making this move, he gently whispered, *Yes, I know you'll miss the house, but remember—I am your dwelling place—not the house you live in or the rooms where you eat and sleep. You'll live in other houses here on earth, but don't get attached to any of them; they are all temporary. I am your permanent dwelling place!*

Checking my Bible when I got back to the house, I read, "Lord, you have been our dwelling place throughout all generations" (Psalm 90:1 NIV). Yes, that was definitely God I'd heard while strolling around the block! Fortunately, I had no idea how many other houses he was referring to. When we moved again awhile back, for the twelfth time, storing some furniture and giving our children other pieces, I heard God's gentle reminder once more: *I am your dwelling place.*

Listening to God and hearing his short message of grace transformed my attitude about moving, and I've had plenty of practice to apply what I've learned. Yet it makes me grateful too for the home he's making me in heaven—where I'll never have to pack again.

Praying through Your Busy Day

It's easy to be distracted in our hectic, fast-paced world so that we miss out on being connected to God. He's always there, but we need to make the effort to connect with him. Here are some suggestions for how you can do that even when your schedule is overflowing.

Making Space to Listen to God

Henri Nouwen once said that we need to create room in our lives for God to do or say something we hadn't planned or scheduled. When we become too hurried to partake of the Bread of Life, he said, we get burned out and depleted.

One of the ways I create space for God is to sit in the quiet sunroom on the back of our house. The room looks out on the trees in the backyard, and one morning as I was there, gazing at our bird habitat (a birdbath and a collection of bird feeders hanging from iron hooks and tree limbs), yellow, purple, and black-and-white birds fluttered around the yard. Tiny goldfinches flitted from branch to branch. Blazing red cardinals, persistent woodpeckers, and chattering blue jays competed for a place at the feeders and suet blocks. Doves fluttered in and feasted on the sunflower seeds scattered over the ground. The variety of winged creatures astounded me, each one different and beautiful in its own vibrant way.

But that's only in my backyard, and those are only a few of the many species God made. Yet even looking at this microcosm, I was struck by the incredible variety of beauty he had created in the world around us.

When you pause a few minutes amid the crazy busyness of your day and look around you—whether it's to enjoy the birds feeding in your backyard, to watch the sun set over the mountains, or to marvel at the softness of a newborn baby's skin—you see the incredible variety of beauty God has created in the world. How amazing that the same God who hung the stars and the moon in the heavens and made every other creature on earth also formed each of us humans uniquely for his purposes; remember this, and you can't help but be filled with awe. The evidence of his creative power is all around us and through us, and it's a marvelous thing to behold.

Make space to listen and see the everyday blessings he gives you in those sacred moments with him, and it will do wonders for your being; in that time and place you may find room to breathe deeply, to laugh or to cry, as you find your rest in him.

Another way to make space to listen is to take a listening walk, where you stroll around a familiar path in your neighborhood intent on listening to the Lord's voice rather than focusing on your own petitions. Or make your drive to or from work a time set aside to listen to God.

As you embark, say something like little Samuel did: "Speak, for your servant is listening" (1 Samuel 3:10 NIV), or pray, "Jesus, you said that your sheep would hear your voice. I'm zipping my lip right now so I can wait upon you and listen to you." Then be expectant.

For those of us with spiritual attention deficit disorder (ADD) who have trouble being still, listening while walking or driving can really help us open up to the voice of the Spirit. You may only hear silence for a while, but if you persist in making time and space to listen to what God has to say to you, he'll be faithful, and you'll be blessed by the voice of the Spirit within.

Start Small

Scripture says not to despise the day of small beginnings (see Zechariah 4:10 TLB). If you are new at making space and time for listening to God, let me encourage you to start with a small amount of time, even just five minutes. Pour out your burdens, your worries, and your petitions (see 1 Peter 5:7), and then be quiet. Silently read a psalm to help center your mind on God if your thoughts wander. Ask God a question. If a priority item on your to-do list pops up, jot it down and go back to listening. Time yourself if necessary, and then commend yourself for making a start. Even five minutes for silence is a great beginning. Then your listening time can grow to ten or twenty minutes or more as you get more comfortable in his presence.

If you find, during those five minutes of intended silence, that your inner thoughts go crazy thinking of everything you have to do or stuff you're worried about, consider yourself totally normal. In the next chapter, I'll share ideas about the way God created our internal "wiring" so that we can connect more easily with him—even those of us who have trouble just *being* because we're so busy *doing* most of the time.

Wherever you are on your prayer journey, take heart. God is waiting to reveal himself to you. He is waiting to speak to you, and he longs for you to come to him. And as Margaret Therkelsen, author of *Realizing the Presence of the Spirit*, says of this process, "The more we are emptied of ourselves as we wait before God, the more he deepens our capacity to receive from him. . . . It is amazing how marvelously God will guide, direct, and accompany Christians through circumstances. . . . He has spread a banquet table for us. How pitiful it is to live on bread and water when milk and honey could be ours!"[6]

When God Says, "Go"

When the Lord directs you to call a certain person, to change a habit, or to yield to him in an area of your life, just do it. Don't wait to see the whole blueprint; don't postpone obedience until all the details are worked out. Follow the light guiding your footsteps. God will do more than you could ask or think. But get moving. Obey.

Going where God sends you may take you out of your comfort zone, but your life will never be boring; it will be a continual adventure. And know that it's never too late to start obeying God; he longs to reveal his plans to a willing heart, no matter what age it is. For example, Lois, a Seattle woman, thought she felt the Lord's call to do his work overseas, but it was too hard for her to leave her family and friends. Later, after becoming a widow, she heard God tell her he wanted her to go to the Philippines. Lois was seventy-six by then, and at first she told him, "I'm too old to go." But eventually she sold all she had and entered into the biggest adventure of her life, becoming the lifeline for many orphans and building an orphanage called "King's Garden."[7]

Just as God had plans for Lois, he also has plans for you. Seek out ways you can listen for his voice, and he will guide you every step of the way because you "are His workmanship, created in Christ Jesus for good works, which God prepared beforehand so that we should walk in them" (Ephesians 2:10 NASB).

Ask for God's help

If listening is difficult for you, pray a prayer like this: "Lord, listening is hard for me. So often I'm talking and doing instead of waiting in silence for your Word. Please help me. Teach me through your Spirit to hear your voice clearly, and grant me faith to obey. Amen."

Even when your life is spinning around you, you *can* find joy through obedience; you *can* gain the inner peace and experience the intimacy with God that your parched soul longs for.

He is waiting for you.

QUESTIONS FOR DISCUSSION AND JOURNALING

1. Which person in this chapter do you identify with most? Me, on one of my frazzled days? The mother whose little boy was trying to tell her something that was important to him? Lois, who got a second chance to obey God? What does your choice tell you about your listening skills?

2. Think back to a time when the Lord spoke to you and you were listening and obeyed. What was the message? What was the result? How did it affect your direction, your attitude, or a

relationship you were in? Was there a time when God spoke to you to do something and you resisted? What was the outcome?

3. Look up these verses: Ephesians 2:10, 1 Peter 1:14, Acts 5:29, and 2 Chronicles 16:9. What do they say about the importance of being obedient to God?

4. In what ways would you like to see changes in the listening, or "contemplative," aspect of your prayer life? What could you do to see that change become a reality?

8

Getting Out of the Box:
Finding Your Spiritual Pathway

Stillness has to do with seeing . . .
the opening our eyes to another dimension,
to the mystery of God that lies all about us.

—M. Mayne

Be still? Are you kidding?" Melissa remarked when we were having a small-group discussion at a conference. "If I'm still, I won't get everything in my Day-Timer accomplished today, and then I might get fired." With a sixty-hour-a-week job, working out at the gym several nights a week, attending her singles' group, looking in on her mom at the assisted-living center, and occasionally getting a good night's sleep, Melissa thought of having moments to reflect or pray as a luxury she didn't have time for.

Being still is a challenge for *lots* of women today. A Connecticut woman told me recently, "Sitting down, being still, and staying awake and conscious is a difficult thing for me. As busy as I am all day, when I finally climb into God's lap to pray at night, I'm so tired I fall right to sleep." As she described it, I thought, *That's not a bad way to fall asleep—in the arms of the Lord.*

I can relate to both of these women. I've had plenty of times when I was going too fast to find quiet moments for prayer—and others when I was so tired that when I finally got stationary, I immediately dozed off. Coming into stillness to connect with God has been a long and steep learning curve. But as I've gotten out of the box of how prayer "has to be," according to "the rules," I've found freedom to enjoy his presence wherever I am and whatever I'm doing.

That old box of rules specified things like sitting in the same chair, in the same place, in the same time every day for my prayer time and using the same specific steps to cover all the bases so I remembered to say all the things I needed to say. Instead, I've learned to tap into the spiritual pathways God has created in me to relate to him, and what I've learned has given me the freedom to totally enjoy his presence.

Connecting with God through Music

God has "hard-wired" human beings so that each one of us has different ways to connect with him. We need to take advantage of our unique spiritual pathways that help us turn down the world's volume and center on the Lord.

As a music lover, I've found that certain music has a soothing and calming effect on me and helps me connect with God. When I set aside time to spend with him and my thoughts jumped around to many other things—*What deadlines or meetings do I have today? What am I going to fix for dinner? Who do I need to call?*—there's a song I sing that never fails to draw me closer to God's heart. I learned the song from missionaries in Thailand. Its words, inspired by Zephaniah 3:17, go like this:

> Quiet me with your love, Lord,
> Quiet me with your love.
> Take my sorrow and shame,
> My fears and my pain,
> And quiet me with your love.

As I close my eyes and sing this little chorus, it calms my heart and slows my breathing. I also keep the words to worship songs in my Bible, and some mornings I get those out to worship. Other days I use an old hymnal and sing hymns like "What a Friend We Have in Jesus," cherishing the lyrics that say, "What a privilege to carry everything to God in prayer."

After quietly singing even a few verses of a hymn or worship song, peace replaces restlessness, and I'm more able to focus on the Lord and what he has to say to me. "Singing is threefold praying," Saint Augustine once said. And it doesn't have to just take place in church; wherever we are, music can quiet our busy mind and connect our heart with the One who gives us the gift of music, even bringing effective intercession.

Since prayer is communicating with God, singing prayers is a way to facilitate our talk with him. There is an old story about a young French girl who heard music for the first time and cried out, "It's God speaking to us!"

CREATIVE CONNECTIONS

Kelly is a young woman to whom God has given a creative visual imagination, and she purposes to use this gift in a way that glorifies him. When Kelly tries to pray and finds her thoughts distracted or whenever she's in turmoil over a problem, she makes a conscious effort to breathe in slowly. As she does, she pictures white smoke representing God's light—his mercy, grace, and love—going into her. When she exhales, she pictures dark smoke leaving her, taking with it all the things she is struggling with at the time: pride or selfishness, judgment or anger. After taking three or four deep breaths this way, she finds herself more focused, quiet, and at peace. To stay focused on Christ in this prayer exercise, she thinks about one of the Lord's specific names or attributes—such as Wonderful Counselor or Prince of Peace, saying it quietly or meditating on it.

If you are visually oriented, as Kelly is, a good way to begin your prayer time might be to picture yourself curled up on God's lap in heaven's throne room with his loving arms around you as you pour out your burdens.

Or see in your mind's eye that you're a sheep and that the Lord Jesus, your Shepherd, is carrying you in his arms beside quiet waters.

Read Isaiah 40:11 to bring this very biblical word picture into focus, slowing your mental motor and bringing you his peace: "He will feed his flock like a shepherd. He will carry the lambs in his arms, holding them close to his heart." And then read the opening passage of the Twenty-third Psalm: "The LORD is my shepherd. . . . He leads me beside peaceful streams. He renews my strength" (Psalm 23:1–3).

TURNING DOWN THE WORLD'S VOLUME

Nature is one of my favorite ways to draw near and tune into God. When I sit on my sun porch and the sound of the birds and wind in the trees isn't drowned out by a ringing phone or a noisy dishwasher, it helps me connect with God. Quiet walks outdoors have led to some of my most significant experiences of hearing God's voice— even if it wasn't the prettiest or brightest day.

One of those times was when we were living in Maine. The night before, I'd talked to my sister on the phone as she raved over the lush pink and purple petunias and the banks of red geraniums in the park near their house in Dallas. In contrast, when I looked out my window, I saw only barren trees and grungy snow. The sky was gray . . . again. Though it was April, we still were enduring cold, wintry weather. When I went outside for my daily walk with Lady, my dog, there were few sounds except for the dripping of melting ice from the roof and Lady's paws crunching the snow. In the entire month, there had been only *twenty-four hours* of sunshine. My soul felt as drained and gray as the sky.

As we walked along, I noticed a rosebush that had been severely cut back. Ice was frozen solid around its branches. That forlorn rose bush reminded me of our family. *We've been pruned too,* I thought. *We're two thousand miles away from family and friends. Holmes's building projects are on a downward slide. Our savings are gone, and money is tight. We're going to a church but haven't found a way to be involved. I feel disconnected and useless.*

Then, in the midst of my negative thoughts, God seemed to whisper, *Like the rosebush, you will bloom again and be fruitful if you sink your roots deep into me. This rosebush wasn't cut back by accident. Someone pruned it purposefully so there would be abundant roses next summer. You've trusted me in the good times. Trust me in the winters too!*

God did bring us through that long winter, and as we saw him provide for us again and again, our trust deepened. We developed a hearty attitude of endurance and perseverance as Holmes worked an all-night job at a printing press and I did substitute teaching by day and wrote magazine articles at night. God taught us invaluable lessons, like thanking him for the gift of life itself, for the many family times we had because we just had each other, and for our kids' smiles as they played in the woods behind our house.

By the next spring, though we still faced difficulties, we were back home in Oklahoma. Eventually, Holmes had construction projects going, and God opened new doors for me in writing and speaking. Slowly, almost imperceptibly at first, the blossoms began to reappear in our lives. As surely as God had promised, summer came again into our lives.

FOCUSING THROUGH JOURNALING

Years ago I began writing in a journal, creating poems, making observations, recording ideas, pouring out my thoughts and my sad and happy feelings, and writing my prayers. I didn't write every day—I'm not that compulsive—but I did write often. Sometimes I have asked God a question in my journal—and then later, when I sensed his answer, I've recorded it. Maybe I didn't get the answer that day or the next, but eventually the light would dawn on the issue. I found that recording my prayers in a journal helped me tune out the tasks I faced and focus on the Lord and what he had to say to me. For me, writing is thinking, and writing out my prayers became a wonderful way to focus my thoughts toward God and parachute down from the frantic pace.

For example, one day last year, during one of the most difficult years of our thirty-five years of marriage, I was discouraged and at a very low point. I verbalized my hurt and distress at our situation and then wrote, "All I can say, Lord Jesus, is please help me experience you in a real way in this dark tunnel so that I'll know—not just with my head but with my heart and mind—and really experience you in the midst of this trial. You said you would never leave me or forsake me. I need you desperately; I need to know you as my husband, my provider, my comfort, and refuge."

Although I kind of hope my sons and daughter don't read my journals after I'm gone (because they'll think, *All Mom did was struggle!*), I know the Lord reads my journal because he answered this prayer day after day, giving me hope and drawing me to experience his strength and grace in the midst of a tough time. I believe God gives us the gift of writing and the opportunity to journal our prayers as a way to connect with him.

Bill Hybels calls writing prayers part of the RPM-reduction program (i.e., slowing down our motors) and says, "Journaling, then, is the important first step in slowing down to pray. It gives the body a brief rest. It focuses the mind. It frees the spirit to operate, if only for a few minutes . . . it's the first step in the right direction."[1]

If journaling your prayers helps you connect and get ready to hear from God, let me encourage you to take time to do it. Cindy, a busy pastor's wife and Christian life director, shared with me that she knows writing down her prayers in a journal helps her draw closer to God's heart. Something about writing her prayers helps her zoom in and focus; it slows down her thinking processes enough to be receptive to the Spirit in a different way than just saying her petitions and concerns. But on some extra-hectic days, she just doesn't take the time to journal after she finally gets her Bible reading done, prays for the women on her staff, and prepares for the day, and when that happens she misses the close connection. If writing your prayers as Cindy or I do feels like drudgery to you, don't feel guilty or think you have to do it just because it works for four out of five people you know. Find out how *you* connect best with God, then do it.

DIFFERENT WAYS TO PRAY

With prayer, there is plenty of room for individual style. Based on the prayers recorded in Scripture, the Lord responds to many stylistic variations from his pray-ers. The fact that we desire to communicate with him matters more to him than how we talk to him. In the Bible, people prayed in various ways: sometimes with hands raised (see Psalm 28:2), sometimes kneeling (see Luke 22:41), or sometimes kneeling with their eyes lifted to heaven (see 1 Kings 8:54). At other times prayers were accompanied by singing (see Acts 16:25). There were prayers without words, silent prayers that were powerfully answered (1 Samuel 1:12–15), shouted prayers (see Joshua 6:16–20), and prayers that were sung to God, like those recorded in the Psalms.

The pray-ers in the Bible didn't just pray at home. They changed locations, sometimes praying on mountaintops (see Exodus 19), inside and outside the temple (see Luke 1:8–10), in prison cells (see Acts 16:23–25), and even from inside a fish (see Jonah 2:1)! There are so many different places we can pray, and wherever we are, we know God is there too. He hears us whether we're in the doctor's office, walking through the neighborhood, confined to a wheelchair or sickbed, riding in the car, doing chores at home, or sitting in our favorite rocker by the window.

God is wonderfully gracious and creative in all the varied ways he allows us to talk to and listen to him. "Any place where we are really alone with God can be for us the secret of his presence," said Andrew Murray.[2] He communicates with us through music, poetry, sermons, and through creation. For many of us, reading the Bible, God's Book, is a great vehicle for hearing his voice; if you want God's direction for your life, it's essential.

Some people, like my oldest son, Justin, connect best with God when they're jogging or rock-climbing; for Justin that means it's just him and God, out in the elements. "The more senses I involve, the more I can stay focused in prayer," an outdoorsy young woman told me. "Hearing the outdoor sounds, feeling God's wind rushing over me, smelling the freshly mowed grass, seeing the wonders of the morning . . . all contribute to connecting more intimately with the Lord," she said.

Sometimes God even speaks in significant ways through our dreams. Interestingly, many Muslims today who come to Christ report his speaking to them and appearing to them in their dreams.

In early fall of 2002 (before the Iraq War started), Jill Boyce, a Dallas woman, felt a burden for the U.S. troops and began to pray for the soldiers—even though she didn't have a son or loved one serving in the military. One night during that season, she had a very disturbing dream. In it, she was standing in the Iraqi desert as a terrible battle raged between American soldiers and the enemy. Scores of U.S. soldiers were wounded, and many were killed. It was the most vivid, heart-stopping dream Jill had ever had, and she prayed earnestly that it wouldn't come true.

The next day another image came into her mind—a camouflage bandana with Psalm 91 written down the middle of it. The thought came to her that if the troops carried the Psalm 91 bandanas, literally "wearing the Word," perhaps many of those casualties she had seen in her dream could be prevented.

Eventually, with the inspiration and help of a military chaplain, Jill produced Psalm 91 camouflage bandanas and had the first batch ready to distribute to soldiers deploying from Fort Hood, Texas, when the war started in March 2003. By summer she had enough money by using her tax refund to give away more than three thousand bandanas to other deploying troops. Now they are available and sold all over the world in PXs and through Jill's Web site, www.psalm91bandana.com, and she directs a foundation that provides free retreats to support and encourage military families. Because God spoke and Jill was listening and obeyed, countless soldiers and their families have been blessed.[3]

Make Time for God

A silver-haired missionary I met in Maine advised me, "Don't pray when you feel like it. Make time for God—schedule an appointment with him and keep it." As busy women, we have appointments with associates at work or we schedule a meeting with girlfriends for lunch or we have a regular date night with our husband. I have three friends who are all just as busy as I am, and if we didn't coordinate our schedules to meet for a quarterly lunch to celebrate our birthdays, we might not see each other at all.

Finding a regular time to be with someone nurtures our relationship, and it's the same with God. But the time of day or night that's best for prayer may be different for different people. Morning has usually been considered the time best suited for prayer and personal worship, Andrew Murray observed in *The Inner Life,* quoting Psalm 5:3: "My voice shalt thou hear in the morning, O LORD; in the morning will I direct my prayer unto thee, and will look up" (KJV).

I love to begin my day by taking time to read the Bible and connect with God in prayer, before all the responsibilities and demands rush in and hijack my attention. But if I'm keeping a grandchild overnight, my prayer time may happen later in the day or when I'm alone at night. Uninterrupted time during the "morning watch," as the classic Christians of old called it, is of great value. But sometimes the morning quiet time becomes an end unto itself, a badge of honor we display out of vanity to our family members, or a religious activity that is done more for show than for the purpose of getting closer to God.

Oswald Chambers reminded us to not allow the way we structure our devotional life to become what we worship or focus on. "Your god may be your little Christian habit, the habit of prayer at stated times, or the habit of Bible reading. Watch how your Father will upset those times if you begin to worship your habit instead of what the habit symbolizes—I can't do that just now, I am praying; it is my hour with God. No, it is your hour with your habit." Instead, our focus needs to be on being at home with God anywhere we are, Chambers said.[4]

Years ago a woman named Maria and her family joined a new church, seeking out a good youth group for their son. She was struck by the contrast between her old congregation and the new church—

it seemed everyone in the new congregation was faithful to rise early and spend extra time with God. "What did you hear in your quiet time today?" or "I had a great quiet time today. Did you?" were common topics of conversation.

What a godly group of people! Maria thought. She realized that to be a godly person herself she had to religiously set aside the early part of her day for prayer.

Since she was a full-time caregiver to a critically ill child, she lost several hours of sleep each night taking care of her daughter. But she had come to think that, in order to be the woman of faith God had called her to be, she had to rise early for her quiet time like all the other people at church.

So Maria faithfully set her alarm and rose early. But day after day, to her disappointment, in less than thirty minutes she'd find herself sprawled over her Bible asleep. As she continued to fail at her prayer time, she let guilt and condemnation flood in. *What a disappointment I must be to God,* she thought.

Then, a few Sundays later in the morning church service, several leaders of the church came forward and asked visitors to leave. A scandal had erupted at the church; there were mean-spirited accusations resulting in a bitter church split. Over the next few months, Maria grew increasingly confused. The people she had highly esteemed as examples were no longer leaders she wanted to follow. She learned, once again, that her focus needed to be on God and how *he* led her.

The Lord never did lead Maria to a 5:30 a.m. quiet time in the years she was caring for her child, but she experienced many intimate moments with him. And she learned as the years went by that people who exemplified Christ the most didn't need to wear a badge that asked, "I had my quiet time today. Did you?" They just mirrored Jesus and made her thirsty for him.

Thereafter, whenever she heard anyone say that Christians must seek God first thing every morning, Maria would reflect on her life, acknowledging that she's a night person, not a morning person. And God gave her the special assignment of being the parent of a critically ill child who was totally dependent upon Maria for her care. Maria's heart seeks God all day, but it is the evening that is her most productive time with him. It's the time she hears him the best, and by going to bed to read and meditate on his Word, she prepares her heart for the next day. Maria knows she doesn't fit into the box that many try to fit her into. As she's grown in Christ, she has found herself becoming less intent on following mankind's rules but flourishing as she operates in the way God fashioned her.

Praying through Your Busy Day

What unique spiritual pathways bring *you* closest to God? Are you a traditionalist who finds mornings the best time for prayer and Bible study, or are you a night owl whose standing appointment with God often comes after midnight? If you're having trouble making time for him, make sure you're not boxing yourself in and abiding by artificial "rules" that have nothing to do with your relationship to your

Creator. Consider these ideas for how you might be more creative in discovering the best way to connect your heart with God's.

Be Flexible

As women, our life is made up of seasons. Having time to commune with God one on one is vital, but it may change as our life evolves through the seasons. I've found that no matter how busy my day is, if I have the *desire* to be with God and if I ask for a window of time to spend with him, he's faithful to show it to me.

When my friend Janet's kids were young, she tried to schedule a consistent early quiet time, but her house was anything but quiet in the mornings and her daily schedule was anything but consistent! So when the days seemed out of control with sick children and sleepless nights, she looked for other opportunities to have time with God. She had some wonderful moments with the Lord as she nursed her baby or during her kids' nap time. Now that her children are older—two of them are even in college—it's much easier to spend time with the Lord earlier in the day.

Catherine, who is retired now, has found that if she is very troubled about something, she'll sleep for a few hours and then get up and go downstairs by herself, sit by the wood stove, and journal her prayers in the middle of the night.

Carol has been caring for her aging mom in her home, and the early morning is filled with countless tasks and interruptions. Before she leaves for work, she has to prepare breakfast for her mother, get everything ready for the shifts of nurses, and get showered and dressed for her workday. Medical supplies are dropped off early by a delivery service, and the first nurse comes before 8:45 a.m. There's little hope for Carol to find quiet time during the mornings. By nighttime, she's exhausted. But she has found that taking time during her hour-long lunch break is one of her best opportunities to read the Bible and tune in to God's voice.

Now that Marie has a forty-five-minute commute each way from her home to the Connecticut church where she serves as women's ministry director, her car is a special sanctuary where she meets with God. As she plays quiet worship music instead of turning on talk radio, Marie finds that during her drive time God gives her guidance and wisdom, even specific scriptures she can use to minister to the women she will meet with that day.

Try Praying in Different Postures

Break up your routine and pray in different ways. I've found kneeling has many benefits, such as reducing distractions and helping me focus. The biggest benefit, however, is that "it reminds us who's who in the dialogue. Prayer is not a couple of fellows chatting about the Dallas Cowboys. It is a human being coming face to face with his or her Supreme Authority, the ineffable God who is approachable but still very much the One in charge," says Dean Merrill.[5] Pray kneeling for a week and see if it gives you more of a sense of humility before God.

If you're sitting at your computer, God would love to hear your voice from that position as well. Pray lying facedown on the floor, or as college kids I know say, "sucking carpet." Or pray with your hands raised and your eyes open instead of closed.

Learning to "sign" a prayer with the deaf sign-language can help you communicate with God through your hands.

Praying in one of these different postures can refresh your prayer life, as can a change of location. The palette of prayer styles is as expansive as the God to whom we speak; he is able to encompass and accept our individuality, no matter how unusual or common it is. From unintelligible groans to whispered petitions to shouted praise, God hears and receives our prayers.

Discover *Your* Spiritual Pathway

Our city installed something called temporary "traffic-calming devices" in an attempt to slow drivers on a street near us where three different schools are located within a two-mile stretch. Now, driving down the street requires motorists to weave their way through four-foot-tall flexible posts arranged in a serpentine, zigzag, obstacle-course kind of route, so they are forced to slow down to avoid hitting the posts.

We busy women may need to add calming devices to our lives. Think about what helps you to be still enough to listen and to hear God's voice. What if you meditated on one or two verses rather than rushing through a set five-page reading? Does playing a worship CD and singing your prayers usher you into God's presence, or is journaling your prayers more effective? Do you feel closest to God when you get away alone to a place of beauty and experience a vivid sunset or watch the waves move the water at a nearby lake? Or do you, like Mother Teresa, experience the presence of God most closely when you are serving others?

One of the best calming devices God has given us is fasting, which means abstaining from food (or other physical comfort) for a period of time specifically for the purpose of devoting that time to seeking the Lord in prayer and/or in his Word. A good resource for learning more about fasting is Derek Prince's chapters on fasting in *Derek Prince on Experiencing God's Power.*[6]

Put into your lifestyle whatever calming devices you find that help you tune in to God and tune out distractions. Use them to draw near to God in the way he has designed for you, and he'll do his part to draw near to you and bless you with his presence and guidance.

Distinguish the Difference

Part of the process of prayer is learning to distinguish God's voice from other voices or from something you made up on your own. A pastor I heard recently said a young woman came to him and said, "I'm hearing God say to have sex with my boyfriend."

"That's anatomy, not God," the pastor replied.

We can be certain God will not tell us to do things that go against what the Bible says. His Word is truth. That's why renewing your mind regularly by reading the Bible is an important way to tune your ears to God's voice (see Romans 12:2). The better you know the Bible and the more securely his Word is hidden in your heart, the more you'll be able to discern whether you are hearing God or the enemy, your own flesh or the world's opinions.

I find it helpful to reflect on a verse that stands out in my daily reading and then say it aloud a few times to ponder its meaning. Then I pray the verse back to God, asking if he wants to speak to me through this passage.

Avoid praying about people and problems in a rote, mechanical way, and open up to how God may want you to pray. As Jim Cymbala said in *Fresh Power,* "We would do far better if we waited on the Lord and were sensitive to the mind of the Spirit about what to do, what to say, and what not to say as we walk among needy people, broken relationships, and other problems that come our way."[7]

Even asking God, before we start naming our list of petitions, "What do you want me to pray about today?" can help us to not be so overwhelmed with needs that aren't really our concerns. Then, once you know what or who you need to bring to God in prayer, ask him:

- What is on your heart, Lord, for this person or situation?
- How do you want me to pray?

If you feel like you have a bit of spiritual ADD at times, ask the Spirit to help you wait quietly so you can hear him. When you are most helpless, he can most help you. And when Jesus fine-tunes your spiritual hearing, you can pray with grace and confidence in whatever way he shows you.

Questions for Discussion or Journaling

1. In what ways described in this chapter could you "turn down the world's volume" to better hear God's voice?

2. In the season of life you're in, when is your most productive time of the day or night to have appointments with the Lord?

3. What spiritual pathway helps you connect with God and hear his voice: being out in nature, moving and prayer-walking, having a time of silence, reading the Bible, singing a song of praise, or some other way?

4. If you wrote your prayers this week, describe how writing them out affected your devotional time and the rest of your day.

9

P-U-S-H! Praying the Distance

*Prayer must often be "heaped up" until God sees that its measure
is full. Then the answer comes: Just as each of ten thousand seeds
is part of the final harvest, frequently repeated, persevering prayer
is necessary to acquire a desired blessing.*

—Andrew Murray

My husband has struggled with a bad habit that is affecting our
marriage. I've prayed for him for over a year, and it hasn't gone away.
I'm so discouraged," a young woman told me.

Have *you* ever prayed and hoped that God would do something
in a situation, as this woman did, and you haven't seen the fruit of
your prayers?

If so, you are in good company. Countless Christians struggle
with this difficulty. We want our prayers to be answered ASAP. We see
complicated crime dramas solved in only one hour and think, *Surely
God can unravel my problem or bring a solution—if not that fast, at least*

within a day or a few weeks. A little part of us hopes God will be like a vending machine. We put in the request and hope the answer will rush down the chute like a can of pop. When prayers aren't answered on our timetable, we get weary or frustrated and are inclined to quit.

But if we understand that the secret to answered prayer is *persistent, prevailing, persevering prayer,* then our attitude becomes more like a marathoner than a sprinter. We aren't just enthusiastic for a few days and then peter out; we're in it for the long haul.

When my daughter-in-law Maggie decided to run the Oklahoma City Memorial Marathon in memory of those in our city who died in the Murrah Federal Building bombing of 1995, she and two friends, Emily and Whitney, trained together. They all taught school, so they met each morning at 5:30 to run. It was hard to get up when it was still dark, especially when it was cold and Maggie was tired, but the women provided great support and accountability for each other during their months of training. And when we cheered them through the twenty-six miles, their smiles showed it was all worth it.

Perseverance in prayer is much like perseverance in sports events. The coach encourages his or her players to *keep trying and not give up,* even when they face huge obstacles, like a stronger opponent or injuries that bench the team's best players.

The truth is, there are some situations where persevering, marathon prayers are necessary so that God's will is done. When Jesus talked about prayer in Matthew 7:7–8, he told us to *keep trying and not give up.* He didn't suggest that we just ask once and give up when we get tired. He said, "Keep on asking, and you will be given what you ask for. Keep on looking, and you will find. Keep on knocking, and the door will be opened. For everyone who asks, receives. Everyone who seeks, finds. And the door is opened to everyone who knocks." What a great promise for those who persevere in prayer!

"But if I pray about something over and over, won't God think I'm nagging? Somebody told me God hates nagging," a young woman asked me at a conference.

"If I pray more than once for a request, doesn't it show I don't have faith?" said another.

On the contrary! Christ encouraged us to keep praying. When he said not to use "vain [meaningless] repetitions" (Matthew 6:7 NKJV), the meaning is that we're not to use prayer as a religious ritual or as a way to attract the attention of others. It doesn't mean we're to pray about something only once. Many stories of the Bible tell of a person who prayed multiple times. Jesus himself prayed three times in the Garden of Gethsemane (see Matthew 26:36–44). Paul asked three times for his "thorn in the flesh" to be removed (2 Corinthians 12:7–9 KJV). And Elijah prayed to God seven times for rain before the drops began to pour from the sky (see 1 Kings 18).

Perseverance in prayer is never nagging. God loves to hear your voice. Just as I've shared how I love to hear my grown sons' voices or the voices of their wives, Tiffany and Maggie, whenever they phone me from another city, and how glad I am to give my daughter the help she needs when she asks, God loves for you to come to him. He *wants* you to ask—and keep on asking him—for the things on your heart. And he promises to personally attend to your request; he won't leave you stuck in a voice-mail wasteland, like the church I called recently.

"Thank you for calling XYZ Church," the automated greeting said. "If you know your party's extension, dial it now. Press 1 for service times. Press 2 for directions on how to get to the church. Press 3 for ministries, 4 for financial assistance, 5 for emergencies, and 7 for upcoming events." There was no way to talk to a person, and when I pressed O to speak to the operator, I got yet another automated voice.

God encourages us to call him—and to call not just once but persistently. Jesus told his disciples (and that includes us as well) a story to illustrate their need for constant prayer and to show them that they must—and we must—"never give up" (Luke 18:1).

His story told of a widow who came to the local judge because someone had harmed her and violated her rights. Day after day she came to ask for the judge's help and protection, but he was a godless man who didn't care about people and least of all, her. So the woman was ignored, denied help, and turned away time after time. But she didn't quit. This was one determined lady! She kept after the judge, doggedly persisting in asking again and again for the help and justice she needed.

"I fear neither God nor man," the judge finally said to himself, "but this woman is driving me crazy. I'm going to see that she gets justice, because she is wearing me out with her constant requests!" (Luke 18:4–5).

Amazing, isn't it? Jesus said for us to be just as relentlessly persistent as that widow. Then he emphasized his point by saying that if even a corrupt judge would give a just decision to a woman he cared nothing about, does it make sense that God, who is full of love and compassion for us, his people, will step in and answer when we persevere in asking (see Luke 18:6–8)?

Then Jesus asked the big question: "How much of that kind of persistent faith will the Son of Man find on the earth when he returns?" (v. 8 MSG). Jesus was saying, "It takes persistent faith for prevailing prayer. Press on! Don't stop praying! Persevere until the answer comes."

It's one of the most important lessons in the school of prayer.

"Every single believing prayer has its influence. It is stored up toward an answer which comes in due time *to whomever perseveres to the end*," said Andrew Murray.[1] Sure, God could answer our prayers immediately. And sometimes he does. But when he doesn't, it may be that he's going to grow our faith and deepen our spiritual roots through our having to persevere, or because he's going to make something bigger and better happen while we wait and pray.

Here's a story that reminds me to persevere in my prayers: A long time ago, a champion swimmer named Florence Chadwick was set to swim the long distance from the California coast to Catalina Island. The conditions couldn't have been worse the day she attempted the swim. The water was freezing, the fog was so thick she couldn't see, and sharks lurked beneath the waves, forcing Florence's trainers to use rifles to keep them away from her. Florence swam for fifteen solid hours. But then she decided she couldn't swim anymore, and she yelled to her trainers to get her out of the water. She was just too tired, too cold, and too discouraged. From her vantage point in the freezing, dangerous waters, the destination seemed too far away.

However, when she got into the boat, she saw that she was only a half-mile from her goal. If Florence had ended there, she would never have succeeded. But that's not the end of the story. Two months later, she tried again. It was still hard, but this time she made it. This time she persevered.

Do you know what happens after a dam is built in a mountain valley? It can take many months (sometimes even a full year) for water to fill the reservoir behind the dam. Drop by drop, day by day, the water gets higher and higher. But when it reaches a certain level, the water begins to turn hydroelectric generators. Then, a huge amount of power is released that can light up a whole city.[2]

Something similar happens when we persevere in prayer. As Andrew Murray explained, to exercise its power, prayer "must be gathered up, just like water, until the stream can come down in full force."[3] As more and more prayers are said for a situation or a person, the prayer "dam" fills up. Then, when it's God's perfect timing, he releases his energy into that situation.

That's why it's so important to P-U-S-H, to **p**ray **u**ntil **s**omething **h**appens! Hold on until the answer comes. Perseverance in prayer really pays off.

Look at the story of persistent Hannah, who spoke the first prayer by a woman ever recorded in the Bible. Hannah had a husband who loved her—Elkanah—and apparently plenty to eat, so he thought she should be happy.

But her deep desire for a child had been thwarted by infertility, and she had had to watch as his other wife, Peninnah, bore Elkanah several children. (It would be reason enough to be miserable if you had to share your husband with another woman in the house, let alone if that woman gave him a large family and you couldn't.) Daily Peninnah provoked and ridiculed Hannah.

"What use did she make of this daily torment? She prayed unto the Lord; she rose up and went forward that she might pray mightily before God; she spoke in her heart and she poured out her soul before God," said Joseph Parker.[4]

Year after year Hannah's tears expressed volumes to the Lord, and in one of the family's annual trips to worship and sacrifice to God at the temple, she poured out her desperation and longing to him once again.

In deep anguish and tears, Hannah said, "O LORD Almighty, if you will look down upon my sorrow and answer my prayer and give me a son, then I will give him back to you. He will be yours for his entire lifetime, and as a sign that he has been dedicated to the LORD, his hair will never be cut" (1 Samuel 1:10–11).

Her groanings were so deep that no words came even though her lips moved. Thinking she must be drunk, the priest Eli accused her of debauchery. But when he discovered her true intent, Eli gave her his blessing and asked God to grant her request. In nine months, Hannah's first son, Samuel, was born. Her persistence and fervency had been rewarded. And true to her word, she offered her little son to God's service when he was old enough to be weaned, and he became one of the greatest men of his time, God's chosen spokesperson and judge over his people.

"Prevailing in prayer until God's answer is given involves the investment of time. Any prayer answer worthy of prevailing prayer is worth all the time you can invest in it. It may involve time spent in prayer on repeated occasions as well as a priority on your heart, so that you return to this special petition whenever you have free time," said Wesley Duewel.[5]

Persevering Prayer Makes All the Difference

What keeps us praying when the goal looks impossible? It's that persistent faith Jesus was talking about in Luke 18. Having faith in the promises of God and maintaining confidence as we praise him that he is able and nothing is impossible for him[6] can make a big difference in our lives—and in the lives of our children. When a family perseveres in prayer, God works in marvelous ways, and the children often become pray-ers themselves, as this true story shows.

Every year that Greg and Martha Singleton's children, Annie and Matt, were in the public schools in their Texas community, Mom, Dad, and the kids would go to the campuses each of them would attend that year and do what they called a "Jericho March" on the night before school started. The whole family would walk around the school, praying for the students and their families, the administrators, and the teachers, and for the family members' witness and ministry among those people. They did this Jericho March not just once or twice but every single year throughout the two kids' elementary and junior high years.

Because both of the Singleton children ended up attending the high school where their mother, Martha, taught, that meant that by the time Matt got to high school, he had been praying for the school *since he was five years old.*

On the night before his freshman year, Matt stood by the flagpole and asked God to make salvation "spring from the ground" at his high school. Things didn't look that promising on the outside. There weren't a lot of active Christians and Christian groups at the school. But he and his family kept praying.

As a member of the freshman football team, he wanted to be part of the Fellowship of Christian Athletes (FCA), but there was only one other student interested in being a member and no coach-sponsor. However, a change in the coaching staff the next year brought a coach who agreed to sponsor the club, with the understanding that, in this public school, every meeting and activity had to be entirely student-initiated and student-led.

Amazingly, in Matt's junior year, there were 275 teens at See You at the Pole—the most ever that attended this nationwide event in which students gather around their school's flagpole on a designated morning in September and pray for their school. Matt and another student led the gathering, and in closing they said, "If you're here and you have never asked Jesus to be your personal Savior, and want to— you can come up here, and we will pray with you." Immediately, thirteen kids stepped up to the flagpole.

As Matt finished high school over the next two years, he served as huddle leader of FCA, assisted by other football players who'd come to know the Lord at school and were growing strong spiritually. The meetings grew to a weekly attendance of forty to eighty teens, with a membership of over two hundred, including both athletes and non-athletes.

In that time, during gatherings held in a meeting room with windows looking out on the flagpole area, well over 100 kids made first-time public commitments to Christ, and 150 others recommitted in a serious way. At the FCA meetings, students of all races and economic backgrounds prayed together and hugged and supported each other. Together they impacted the whole student body. The principal said the high school had become a different place in those four years, and teachers and parents noticed the change as well.[7]

Great changes can occur in our homes and in our communities when we persist in prayer, cling to God's promises, give him time to work, and *pray until something happens.*

Praying through Your Busy Day

I hope this chapter has helped you grasp the importance of being persistent in your prayers and that it has inspired you to press on in your petitions and keep praying until something happens. Here are a couple more ideas to get you started—and keep you going.

Make a List

What helps you continue in prayer? For me, a five-by-seven index card where I write my prayer list is a simple but powerful tool to persistently intercede for those on my VIP list: my husband, our adult children and their spouses, our five grandchildren, other family members and friends who have health problems, and several young men serving in Iraq and Afghanistan.

I jot down their names with either a word or two to remind me of their greatest need or with a Scripture verse I am praying for them. Then I tuck the card into my Bible so it will be before me every day. For example, for Justin and Tiffany I wrote this week, "Faith + Hope = Trust" to remind me what to pray for them as they consider Justin's next assignment with his international corporation, which will move them again in a few months. I pray that they will be in agreement with each other and with God in their decision.

For my husband, Holmes, I wrote Psalm 67:1 to remind me to ask God to bless him and that God would make "his face shine with favor" upon Holmes at his work. For our son Chris (and his wife, Maggie) during his deployment, I noted Psalm 91 and other verses. For Alison and her husband, I wrote Romans 12:10 so I would remember to ask God that they would love each other "with genuine affection and take delight in honoring each other." (It's a great prayer for a marriage.) For our grandchildren I wrote John 3:16, to ask that they would receive and love Jesus as their Savior from an early age.

I make a new list each month, and I write "thank you" next to the requests on the old card, expressing gratefulness aloud for each one where the answer has been seen or experienced. I'm amazed, as I review the cards from past seasons that I keep in a separate folder, how many of my prayers God has answered.

Pray with Others

One of the most dynamic things we can do to persevere in prayer for a long-term need is to pray with other people. We don't have to be Lone Ranger pray-ers; we aren't meant to be. It is very hard to persevere in prayer when you get discouraged and are all alone. When the Singleton family gathered to pray for the schools Annie and Matt would attend and Martha would work at, their united prayers together had even greater power than if only one of them had prayed. Matthew 18:19–20 clues us in on this secret. Your prayers are already effective, Jesus was saying, but combine them with others, and the power increases: "When two of you get together on anything at all on earth and make a prayer of it, my Father in heaven goes into action. And when two or three of you are together because of me, you can be sure that I'll be there" (MSG).

That "two or three" could be you and your prayer partner connecting with God and each other on the phone, or you and a prayer group, a husband and wife, a mom and a daughter, or like the Singletons, your whole family. Our burdens are lightened when we pray about them with others. As we gather, we impart staying power, hope, and strength to each other so we can keep praying until something happens.

When God's Spirit harmonizes our prayers and we see his answers, we get motivated to keep praying. Prevailing in prayer with others also strengthens our walk with Christ and our faith in his power.

I have experienced that truth week after week as fifteen or more women come to my home for an hour of prayer. Each of us has various concerns for our sons and daughters who are in colleges and careers spread all over the United States and the world. One mother was praying her son through his recovery from an addiction. Another was undergirding her son through four long years of medical school and residency. They prayed with me for our son during his two deployments in less than two years. Many of them have been praying for years for their children's spouses, who have not come on the scene. All of us are strengthened by our weekly, continuing prayer together. And if one mother's prayer hasn't been answered yet, she is encouraged by how God is working in another mother's situation.

Even the great leader Moses needed help to persevere in prayer. Exodus 17 tells how the Israelites, led by Joshua, went out to fight the army of Amalekites who had attacked them. As Joshua led his men into battle, Moses, Aaron, and Hur went to the top of a nearby hill so they could see the action.

As long as Moses held up his staff with his hands—a symbol of his praying for the army—Joshua and the Israelites were winning the battle. But as the day wore on and he grew tired, he lowered his hands, and the Amalekites gained the upper hand, defeating and killing God's people. Since Moses was too tired to hold up the staff any longer, Aaron and Hur brought a stone for him to sit on. They stood on each side of Moses, holding his hands up until sunset, when the battle was completely won and the army of Amalek was defeated.

Each of us needs our own Aarons and Hurs in the spiritual battles we face; we can be that kind of prayerful support for one another.

Even if you become tired or think that things will never change, don't stop praying. Call others to come alongside you to pray with and for you. Find a prayer partner who is trustworthy and will hold your requests confidentially, sharing them only with you and the Lord. It could be an older woman you could pray with regularly. As a young mother, one of the kindest things God did for me was provide Flo Perkins, who welcomed me and a small group of other young women to her home at 5:30 a.m. once a week to pray. Flo had been going into God's presence in prayer for more than fifty years, and to her it was as natural as breathing. This wonderful prayer partner just took us in under her wings. I learned a great deal about prayer from praying with Flo, and I was inspired by her perseverance and her love for others. If you don't have a group to pray with, ask God to send you friends to support you.

Drop by drop, keep filling the prayer bowls with your requests. It may be only a thimbleful that you add today with your prayers, but as you do, remind yourself of God's faithfulness and thank him in advance for how he's going to work. Trust his wisdom and timing, and be sensitive and open to his guidance. I've experienced times when I'm chugging away, persevering in prayer for something and then sensed God saying to me, "It's done. You can begin to thank me now instead of continuing to ask," or "You need to pray in a different direction. Here's what's on my heart for this situation, this person."

If we're paying attention to the Holy Spirit and our hearts are open and yielded, God will light our path of prayer, shift our focus, or stir us to thank him in advance. But one thing is certain: he will be faithful!

As the Bible tells us, "Don't get tired of doing what is good" (and we know that prayer is good). "Don't get discouraged and give up, for we will reap a harvest of blessing at the appropriate time" (Galatians 6:9).

Keep praying; the "appropriate" time for your need may be just around the corner.[8]

QUESTIONS FOR DISCUSSION OR JOURNALING

1. As you read this chapter, did a situation or person come to mind that you realized you'd lost hope for and had stopped praying for? If so, let me encourage you to be honest with God about the issue. Write down the prayer request, and just as swimmer Florence Chadwick did, return to the situation and this time go the distance in praying on it.

2. This chapter lists several benefits of praying with others and also cites ways it helps us persevere in marathon prayers. What are three of those benefits? If you've experienced any of them, share with others in your group.

3. What do Psalm 22:1–5 and Hebrews 11:6 tell us about God?

4. How do you feel when you're in the "waiting room"? What do you need most in that "place" to persevere and wait patiently for the answer?

5. Who are your prayer partners? Who taught you the most about prayer?

10

Praying on the Spot

There is always a suitable place to pray, to lift up your eyes to God; there is no need to get to a place of prayer; pray wherever you are.

—Oswald Chambers

W_e were on the second leg of a flight from Dallas–Fort Worth International Airport to Seattle. Holmes and I settled into our emergency-row seats, fastened our seat belts, and opened our magazines as we waited for the plane to begin its taxi to the runway. The man sitting next to me had a large, red *One-Year Bible* in his lap, and after he greeted us, a conversation opened up.

On some flights I'm engrossed in a magazine or busy reviewing my notes, but for some reason this man and I struck up a conversation before the plane was even off the ground. His name was John, and he said he had come back to Christ just a few years earlier after a long absence from God after the death of a child and his subsequent divorce. He described how he had begun to read the Bible, found a church, and eventually remarried.

"What are you headed to Seattle for?" he asked, and I explained I was speaking at a conference at a church in the suburbs of the city.

"How about you?" I inquired. Then John began to tell me about his brother Jay, who was in dreadful shape both physically and mentally. After Jay's wife had died of cancer three years before, he had gone downhill, John said. He'd been suicidal earlier and had some serious health problems, so the year before John had gone to get him and had flown with him to his home city in Florida, where John and his wife had cared for him at their house after a stint in the hospital. Then Jay had insisted on going back home to Seattle.

This time John wasn't sure if he could get his brother to go with him, and he was really discouraged. They had a third brother, but he hadn't been able to make any headway with Jay.

"In fact, he goes to the church where you're speaking," John told me. The brother-in-crisis definitely needed medical care, but he was holed up in a motel and had told both brothers over the phone to leave him alone. He said he had nothing to live for.

Actually he had two grown children and a family who cared about him, but his perspective was clouded by severe depression and from failing to take his medication and to eat properly. What concerned John even more was that his brother had been angry with God and had been estranged from him for as long as John could remember.

As I listened to John's story, I felt a nudge to pray for him. We continued to talk, and right before our descent into the Seattle airport, he said, "I'd really appreciate your and Holmes's prayers. I don't know what the outcome's going to be this weekend, but I want to help my brother."

"We'd be glad to pray for you and your brother. What about now?" I offered.

I don't remember everything we prayed. But we all sensed Jesus's presence with us in a significant way as we sat on that plane and asked the Spirit to fill John with strength and hope. We also asked him to open Jay's heart to accept help and to turn to God—while God provided everything John needed for this rescue operation.

On Sunday morning, brother number three came up after the service where I spoke and said he was praising God for bringing us together with his brother on the airplane. "You and Holmes were a very special blessing to John that he needed right at that moment, and God did provide all he needed. John and Jay are on a plane right now heading to John's home," he said.

The next week I got an e-mail from John: "I've been very busy taking care of my brother. My mind seems to be in 'park' from lack of sleep. We arrived back home on Sunday afternoon, and I took him to the emergency room because of swelling in his abdomen. He had reopened his hernia and needed surgery Tuesday morning to repair it. I'm sitting in his room now waiting for a psychiatrist to come. He's in a lot worse shape than I'd imagined. He looks like a ninety-year-old man who has been starved to death. My prayer is that he can regain his sanity so he can have another chance to restore his relationship with God. I've placed Jay in God's hands. Now I just need to keep reminding myself of that and trust him to do what is best. Thank you for being willing to pray for me on the spot; I know those prayers made a difference."

What a privilege it was that day to be a small part of what God was doing in one brother's rescue operation for his sibling. It reminded me of the story told in the Gospel of Mark when Jesus was in a house teaching and preaching, and the crowd grew so big they were "jamming the entrance so no one could get in or out" (Mark 2:2 MSG). Four men had brought their friend, a paraplegic, on a stretcher. But when they couldn't get in through the door, they resourcefully cut a hole in the roof and lowered their friend right in front of where Jesus was standing. Their efforts and faith were rewarded when their friend wasn't just healed but was also forgiven by the Lord and given a brand-new start—just what Jay needed too.

Praying on the spot for people is somewhat like that. It conveys those who have a need right to the One who has the mercy, grace, and power to help. Oswald Chambers wrote, "Prayer is the exercise of drawing on the grace of God. Don't say—I will endure this until I can get away and pray. Pray *now;* draw on the grace of God in the moment of need."[1]

We can be assured the Lord will freely give that help to those who ask.

Overcoming a Barrier

Praying on the spot is also a great way to deal with one of the main struggles busy women have with prayer: being overwhelmed by the quantity of requests that flood in, making them feel unable to remember to pray for them all.

"I've got a big family, and trying to be faithful to pray for all of them and for the girls in my Bible study is about all I can handle," said a thirty-something woman. "I start to feel like I'm 'all prayed up.' Then I meet an acquaintance who asks me to pray for her mother who's just been diagnosed with cancer, and someone at Wednesday night church asks for prayer for her teenage son who is out of control, and one of the kids in the choir I direct says her dad's out of a job and needs prayer. I tell them all that I'll pray for them, but as the needs pile up, I get so overwhelmed I'm paralyzed and I can't pray for any of them. Then the guilt sets in."

How often does someone express a need and ask you to pray for him or her? Do you ever get overwhelmed or lose the slip of paper you wrote the person's name on or stick it in your purse and forget about it? When we're busy, it's easy to let those things happen. Instead, we can offer to pray with that person right there. Five little words—"Could I pray for you?"—may make a big difference in that person's life. I know it did in mine.

It happened a few weeks after my mom died. The memorial service was over, and we had driven back to Oklahoma City. The kids had gone back to their classes, and I had returned to volunteer teaching at their school and helping in my husband's store. I kept busy, but I couldn't shake the painful memories of how cancer had ravaged my mother physically. She'd been only fifty-nine years old when her once beautiful, dark, wavy hair had fallen out due to radiation, her body had become swollen, and pain besieged her constantly. She'd been one of the most energetic people I'd ever known, but for the last month of her life she couldn't get out of bed and struggled even to breathe.

These images weren't the way I wanted to remember my mom. But when I thought of her, only sad memories of those last few months in the hospital came flooding into my mind, compounding my grief. I hadn't really been able to verbalize to anyone how this was really affecting me, but God must have known.

One day when I was getting out of the car to go into our store, The Woodworks, my friend Patty, the owner of a natural-foods store next door to us, was coming out of her place. She came over and put an arm around me.

"Cheri, how are you doing?"

Patty must have seen the look on my face and noticed the tears that welled up in my eyes. I tried to explain how I was feeling bogged down now that we'd gotten back from Texas after completing some of the wrapping-up work we'd had to do at the ranch following Mom's memorial service. With the school's fall activities revving up and Holmes needing me to help at the store, I was struggling to keep up—while still grieving for my mom.

"Could I pray for you?" she asked gently. Oh, what wonderful words those were to a hurting heart. Many people had passed by me at church or in the neighborhood in the weeks before, saying, "How are you?" yet not even staying around long enough to hear the answer. Or they'd called out across the school parking lot, "Hope you're bouncing back and feeling better after your mom's death."

But in that moment, time stopped as Patty asked the Lord to do something profound yet simple; only his Spirit must have revealed it to her. Patty prayed that God would wrap his love around my memories of my mother in her terrible sickness and replace them with memories of her liveliness and beauty.

And do you know? He did just that. Jesus touched me as Patty quietly prayed for me on the curb of that busy street, and I am forever grateful that she took the time out of her schedule to minister to me.

Passing On the Blessing

Praying on the spot isn't complicated or difficult. And it has much precedent among Christians throughout history. It is said that from the time he was a young boy and throughout his life, Smith Wigglesworth, one of the great evangelists of the early twentieth century, would kneel down wherever he was and talk to the Lord.[2] People I know who hosted Corrie ten Boom in their home said that while they were in conversation with her she would look up and listen to God, respond to him, and then seamlessly (not piously, but naturally) go right on with the conversation.

People all around us long for someone who cares enough about them to ask, listen, and pray or bless them. In the months and years since that day when Patty prayed for me on the spot, I've rarely had anyone turn me down when I've gently asked, as she did, "Could I pray for you?"

When a friend calls to tell us about a big need (she wouldn't call long distance to ask for prayer unless it was important), we can ask if we can pray together after she's explained the problem. Jen, a pastor's wife in New England, told me what a lifeline her friend is who lives in another state. They talk almost daily and are very thankful for the unlimited minutes offered by the cell-phone company they both use. They tell each other about their children, their lives, what's going on that week, and what they're struggling with.

Then, before they go, they say, "Now we'll pray, OK?"

Jen said they had prayed through her friend's move out of state, her treatment for and recovery from cancer, problems with their children, and lots more. They e-mail each other verses on a specific attribute of God they're focusing on. So many of their phone prayers have been answered they've started a "God Journal" to record them all. In dry seasons, those answered prayers spur Jen's desire to keep praying on the spot for her friend and for other women she encounters.

My friend from college, Edie, called me as I was in the middle of writing this chapter, asking me to keep her son Bradley in my prayers. Bradley had just called after a doctor's appointment, and the diagnosis was sudden, complete hearing loss in his right ear. I dropped what I was doing to listen carefully as Edie explained what had happened. Then I asked her if I could pray for Bradley with her before we got off the phone. We don't know what the outcome will be for her son, but we know God heard our conversation and our prayers, and that even though we are separated by miles, there's no distance between us and our God, the Creator of time and space.

When You're Working

Praying right in the middle of your workday is very practical for many career women—and which of us isn't working, whether we are married or single, with or without kids? (I love this definition of a working mother: "What every woman becomes the moment she leaves the delivery room.")

My friend Rosemary, a talented artist, prays on the spot when she and her graphic designer hit a computer glitch. As a freelance artist, she often prays that God will provide her with new projects and continued work. Since her divorce many years ago, she has found it true that "unless the LORD builds a house, the work of the builders [or the artist, in her case] is useless" (Psalm 127:1). So she consults the Lord all along the way as she creates, paints, or designs her latest project.

Connie, a Christian psychotherapist and Bible teacher, leads a busy life but finds time to pray on the spot for the many people she sees in her office each day. At the end of each counseling session, Connie takes a few moments to pray with her client. She then pauses to pray Psalm 119:66, asking God to give her wisdom and discernment to help the next client before he or she arrives. Across the hall is a medical doctor in family practice. As Connie sees sick people going into his office, she prays for their health and for God to give the doctor eyes and ears to know what treatment would be best for them.

When she is getting ready in the morning, Connie silently prays for each person on her schedule that day as she showers, dries her hair, and puts on her makeup. When she fills the dishwasher, she prays for her husband's leadership in their home, at work, and in the relationships he has with his employees. She prays for her girlfriends and their lives as she feeds the dog or throws a load of laundry into the washing machine. Before she knows it, the chores are done, and her on-the-spot prayers are complete.

"Even in the midst of my busy days, God gives me 'mini-moments' to lift those around me in prayer," says Connie. "Everyone we come in contact with daily is struggling with something. It may be a job, the marriage, an illness, or stress. Everyone needs our prayers."

As women, we're relational; connections and relationships with people are a priority for us. We tend to be concerned about the people around us at work, in our families, or within our circle of friends—and sometimes we unconsciously carry a burden for their well-being. We wonder, *Are they doing OK? Does he or she need help? Is that person not feeling well today?* Prayer is just a normal, spontaneous response to our awareness of the needs of others. And when we run into something in the midst of our day, we can send a prayer heavenward right then. We don't have to wait until we get home or rely on our overloaded memory that is already full of things we need to do.

PRAYING THROUGH YOUR BUSY DAY

It's so common for us to tell a friend or loved one, "I'll be praying for you" when a problem is shared or a need is expressed. And certainly we want to keep that prayer commitment. But we can also say, "Could I pray for you?" and do it *now*. We can pray on the spot for that person and get our prayer work started before another minute goes by. Here are some more praying-on-the-spot ideas.

One Day at a Time

"There are so many people and things to pray for: my friend who's struggling with MS, a couple I know who are separated, a niece in college, struggling countries, hardworking missionaries, people at church who are ill, ladies in my Bible study. The longer the list is, the more overwhelmed I get," a young woman told me recently.

It's a common complaint. Dena, an active mother of four in Texas who is working on her master's degree, performing on weekends at a local theater, and juggling a lot of other activities, found a way to deal with this situation. She always wanted to pray for requests people gave her but found herself always feeling guilty about not doing enough.

One day she wrote down every prayer request she could think of—for herself, family, friends, church, community, nation, and the world. Then she divided them into thirty-one equal segments, and put them in a notebook. She keeps the notebook in her bathroom, one of the only places where she can count on some moments alone *every* day. Each time she is "on the throne," as she told me with a little pun intended, she brings her requests to the feet of God's throne and prays over the few items that correspond to that specific day of the month. She adds and subtracts prayer requests as needed. That way she prays for the multitude of needs in her world—one day, one minute, at a time. And she's seen God answer these requests in amazing ways.

Having a place to write down specific requests for things God lays on your heart may help you be less frazzled because you know you're not promising God or someone else to pray and then forgetting about it. You could designate Monday as the day you pray for missionaries, Tuesday as prayers-for-family day, Wednesday for friends, Thursday for government and military, Friday for schools and teachers, Saturdays for yourself, etc.

Instead of getting bogged down by taking on every prayer need you hear of, ask God to guide you in taking on the prayer assignments he wants you to be faithful with. When you're yoked with him and his purposes, Jesus promises that your burden will be light, not more than you can handle (see Matthew 11:29–30 KJV).

Pocket Prayers

Short prayers can accomplish great things; praying in the pockets of time we do have can make a big impact. The first time Deana decided to pray for her daughter Ruth during the few minutes they waited together for Ruth's ride to school, her daughter looked at her and said, "Mommy, I like that! Can you do that for me every day before school and even until twelfth grade and college?"

If you receive an e-mail from a friend who expresses a need or a struggle, a loss or a disappointment, consider praying for that person while you're answering his or her e-mail. Include what you're praying in your reply.

Sometimes we think we've got to pray long prayers to get any help from heaven. When you pray for someone or for yourself, don't feel like you have to go on and on; you can pray short, simple, conversational prayers, and God can do wonderful things in response to your succinct request. In the Bible many brief prayers were greatly rewarded. Here are three of my favorites:

- The ten lepers' prayer: "Jesus, Master, have mercy on us!" (Luke 17:13).
- Peter's prayer of "Save me, Lord!" (Matthew 14:30) when he was sinking.
- King Jehosaphat's prayer: "O our God, . . . We do not know what to do, but our eyes are upon you" (2 Chronicles 20:12 NIV).

Amy Carmichael, the English missionary whose Dohnavur Fellowship rescued hundreds of children from tragically abusive situations, encouraged praying short "telegraph prayers," as she called them. She wrote that we all have a continual need for the Lord's help and that he is nearer than we can imagine, "so near that a whisper can reach him." Her habit was to send up little telegraph prayers such as these, and she suggested we do the same in our everyday lives:

- "Thy patience, Lord," or "Thy love, Lord" when she was feeling impatient or unloving.
- "Thy courage, Lord!" when she needed courage.
- "Thy quietness, Lord!" when she needed a quiet mind.

"Shall we practice this swift and simple way of prayer more and more?" Amy asked. "If we do, our Very Present Help will not disappoint us."[3]

Here are some other short but powerful prayers you could pray:

- "Holy Spirit, think through me until your ideas are my ideas." —Amy Carmichael
- "Lord, help my marriage, and begin with me."
- "Grant me the love that covers a multitude of sins" (see 1 Peter 4:8).
- "Your will be done in my life, Lord."
- "Bring him out of darkness into your light," or "Deliver him from evil."
- "Lord, change *me.*"

QUESTIONS FOR DISCUSSION AND JOURNALING

1. What is a short prayer you remember from the Bible or from your own life that was answered, perhaps with great results? It could be a time when you prayed for someone, or someone prayed for you.

2. For whom, or for what situations, do you feel you should consistently be praying for? Which of these situations are concerns God has laid on your heart? Make a list of them, and also list your personal needs and the things and people that are important to you. Then divide them among the days of the week or the month and post them on a prayer calendar; or find some way that is workable for you to regularly pray for these people and situations. After a few weeks, share with your group what has happened, either inside you (in your heart or your attitude) or outside, in the situation.

3. Where is a place you could pray on the spot for someone?

4. What barrier in your prayer life have you overcome?

5. What is a key insight you've gained from this chapter? How could you apply it in the week to come?

11

Praying for Your Enemies:
The Clean-Slate Principle

I learned that if you love your enemies, you touch the ocean of God's love as never before.

—Corrie ten Boom

WHEN MY FRIEND KAREN was a director for a film festival in Los Angeles, she hired an office assistant named Terry. Although Terry interviewed well, before long she was slamming doors, yelling, and ignoring her employer's requests.

Karen's repeated attempts to talk with Terry about her attitude resulted in no changes. Finally one night Terry called Karen at home to complain that she'd had enough of her boss's demands and was so rude that Karen told her, "I've had enough. You don't need to come back to work."

Terry flew into a rage and slammed down the phone.

At first Karen didn't feel anything but anger toward her "enemy." As the days went on, however, her attitude made it hard to pray and harder still to hear God's voice. Eventually, in determined obedience to a Bible passage she'd read in Matthew 5:44—"When someone gives you a hard time, respond with the energies of prayer" (MSG)— Karen began praying for her former employee. As she prayed, she realized she needed to forgive Terry, and with every prayer of forgiveness, her anger dissipated. She sensed there must be a very wounded person behind those outbursts.

Three months and many prayers later, Karen invited Terry to lunch. There she learned about the struggles Terry was dealing with and that Terry had been the victim of severe abuse and neglect while growing up. Both women cried; they experienced reconciliation and amazingly, began a friendship.

Sooner or later, you will encounter a person who rubs you the wrong way, as happened to Karen. Despite your best intentions, another person will become your adversary. Perhaps someone talked behind your back at church, mounted a campaign against you in the PTA, or betrayed or hurt you in other ways. She could be your mother-in-law, a neighbor, or someone in your own house.

We can have a seemingly great relationship with God for a while, but when a sandpaper relationship comes into our life with its accompanying hurts and unforgiveness, our prayer life can take a downward spiral.

As difficult as it is to pray for your "enemy" (not necessarily someone you've had a big fight with but a person who opposes you, hurts you, or that you've had an adversarial relationship with despite your best efforts), here's why it's important to do so.

DRAWING CLOSER TO GOD

A few years ago, I had an unexpected conflict with a woman during preparations for a community event we were both working on. Although I intended no harm, something I said offended Kim (not her real name), and she told me so in no uncertain terms. While I apologized, Kim remained aloof and unfriendly and said hurtful things to others that I eventually heard. God and I had a few conversations about Kim. I would have loved it if he had changed her. In fact, I asked him to do so several times!

Instead, he suggested I pray blessings on her life whenever her name came up in mine. One day I said, "Lord, you could have reconciled us before now. What's up?" His quiet whisper seemed to say, *You wouldn't have come to me nearly so often lately were it not for Kim!* Nothing changed instantly with the relationship, but I realized that praying for her was drawing *me* closer to God.

EXPERIENCING HEART CHANGE

Because of her commitment to prayer, by the time Karen met her "enemy," Terry, for lunch and heard her story, she actually wanted to hug Terry. Three months before, Karen had been nowhere near that response. In following Jesus's command to "pray for our enemies,"

God slowly filled Karen's heart with his love for Terry. Now she felt compassion when all she'd felt before was hurt, anger, and frustration.

In a similar way, I began to feel differently toward Kim as I touched the ocean of God's love for her individually by praying for her. Praying for another person is the most significant way we can love that person and bless his or her life. It's more impacting than a hug, a material gift, or a kind remark (even though each of those things is a way to bless someone).

Seeing God at Work and Finding Forgiveness

When Karen invited God into her rocky relationship with Terry through prayer, he did more than she could have asked or thought, something the Bible mentions in Ephesians 3:20. Through their growing friendship, Terry found a relationship with Christ and today teaches women in Bible studies and has a fruitful ministry and life. And as Karen saw in a tangible way how God could turn a bad situation into something good, her faith was boosted enormously.

When we pray for those who hurt us, besides the possibility of a reconciled relationship, perhaps the most important thing that can happen is that we are led to forgiveness. Jesus says in the Lord's Prayer (see Luke 11:2–4) that by the measure we forgive others, we're forgiven. Praying for those who oppose us teaches us a real-life lesson in forgiveness.

Maybe you have heard that if you have been hurt by someone, you should just start praying for that person and everything will be all better! But you've also got to *forgive* that person, not just pray for

182

him or her. When someone has done a horrible deed, it can be very difficult to forgive, but that's what God is after in our heart.

When Corrie ten Boom was ministering in Germany after the war, she met the cruel guard who'd made her sister suffer terribly as she died in the concentration camp. After Corrie's talk, the guard came up to her and shared the wonderful news that he had found Jesus and had confessed all his sins to him. He quoted 1 John 1:9 to her, that "if we confess our sins, he is faithful and just to forgive us our sins, and to cleanse us from all unrighteousness" (KJV).

Then he asked Corrie ten Boom to forgive him for his cruelties. In her heart she'd had much bitterness against this man for the things he'd done to Betsy. But then she prayed, "Lord Jesus, thank you for Romans 5:5 [which says God has poured his love into our hearts by the Holy Spirit]; thank you that God's love takes away my bitterness."

Then a miracle happened, she said. "It was as if I felt God's love flowing through my arm. I was able to forgive that man and even shake his hand. You never experience God's love more marvelously than at the moment he gives you love for your enemies."[1]

As George Herbert, an English poet, once said, "He that cannot forgive others, breaks the bridge over which he himself must pass if he would ever reach heaven; for everyone has need to be forgiven."

HEALTH IS RESTORED

A vibrant, thirty-something woman came up to me recently at a coffee shop and said, "Would you forgive me? I've held bitterness against you for a long time, and I know now it's wrong. I'm a cancer survivor, and I've found that harboring *any unforgiveness* is deadly to my body as well as to my soul."

"What did I do that offended you?" I asked. I hardly knew her and couldn't remember any negative encounter we'd ever had.

"Once in the parking lot at church you spoke to my friend Debbie but you didn't know my name. That really hurt me and made me angry."

After I apologized for having a hard time remembering names (especially if I've only met the person once; nametags would help!) and spoke the forgiveness she asked me for, she sat down and shared with me her journey from a diagnosis of cancer to health and wholeness. The truth she learned applies to us all: unforgiveness damages us, body, soul, and spirit, but forgiveness and praying for those who hurt us produce life.

Praying through Your Busy Day

Having a clean slate when we come to God in prayer is vital. Jesus said if we come to the altar and realize that someone has something against us, we need to go to that person and be reconciled before we bring our gift or request to God (see Matthew 5:23–24). I've found the following tips help when I'm tempted to harbor resentment or when I'm having conflict with someone.

Take a Time-out

Consider writing down the specific offenses and how they've affected you. Don't try to sugarcoat the situation or your feelings. Then commit the list to God, asking him to heal your heart—and the other person's as well. Whenever a negative thought about the person comes to mind, whether or not it's accompanied with any painful feelings or questions, like, *Why is she so irritating? Why doesn't* she *ask me to forgive* her? *Why do I have to be the one to initiate things?* pray a specific scripture for her. Replace your negative thoughts with God's Word by asking him which passage would best express his heart toward the person.

Confess Your Part

My mom always said it takes two to tango in a conflict. What's your part in the situation? What are some wrong things you've done that are related to your interaction with this person or in other parts of your life that grieve God or violate his Word? It could be judgmental or critical thoughts about her, or giving a bad report about her to others because you're frustrated and can't vent directly to her about it.

God longs to hear from his children, but the lines of communication get clogged up with unconfessed sins such as unforgiveness, judgmental spirit, envy, or bitterness. As the sin builds up, it's harder for us to perceive God. But he hasn't moved!

Psalm 66:18 is a serious verse that we who want to have a real, alive prayer life need to pay attention to: "If I had cherished [or harbored or held on to] sin in my heart, the Lord would not have listened" (NIV). Whoa! If we are holding on to sin and not letting go of it—not confessing our sin and asking God to forgive us—we may as well not pray, because he doesn't hear us.

D. L. Moody expressed it like this: "Unless you humble yourself before God in the dust, and confess before Him your iniquities and sins, the gate of heaven, which is open only for sinners saved by grace, must be shut against you forever."[2] That sounds pretty harsh, but it's true. If you've had difficulty forgiving, or if you sense you have a hard heart, ask for a spirit of repentance. Then say a simple but profound prayer from Psalm 139: "Search me, O God, and know my heart; try me and know my anxious thoughts; and see if there be any hurtful way in me, and lead me in the everlasting way" (vv. 23–24 NASB). You may be surprised at what he shows you.

When the light bulb goes on and illuminates our wrongs, and when we confess them, then the floodgates open up. God gives us a clean slate; he cleanses us from sin and gives us his righteousness. His living water and life flow through us once again. The communication lines open up, and we hear his loving voice directing us. As Cindy Jacobs said, "When we let God strip our hearts of those things that need changing, he will share with us the secrets that the kings speak in their chambers and entrust us to intercede over whole nations."[3] What amazing grace!

Put Feet to Your Prayers

As you pray, listen for any action steps God might tell you to take, and be faithful to obey them. When Elaine found out that Bonnie, a coworker, was spreading lies about her, Elaine went to her knees. Praying each morning before work, she gave God her hurt feelings but also asked him to fill Bonnie with his peace. Bonnie's barbs continued, but when Christmas rolled around several months into the situation, she felt God nudging her to do something kind for the woman. She bought a gift book by Bonnie's favorite artist and gave it to her for Christmas. Slowly the walls between them began to crumble, and eventually Elaine was promoted to a position that took her out of Bonnie's department.

Then, Be Expectant

Jesus declared that when we follow *his* way of dealing with our enemies, we'll never regret it. That's why he tells us, "When someone gives you a hard time, respond with the energies of prayer for that person. . . . Live out this God-created identity the way our Father lives toward us, generously and graciously, even when we're at our worst. Our Father is kind; you be kind" (Luke 6:28, 35–36 MSG).

When Sue and her husband moved across the country for a new pastoring assignment, it was the most difficult time of her life. As the year began, she had determined that her upcoming birthday would mark a life committed to prayer. And it did. She just didn't know the path it was going to take her.

Their move caused them to leave dear friends and rich fellowship. Her health became poor, and their high-school-age daughter began reacting with rebellion to all the changes. Soon Sue found herself in ICU on the brink of death; after a transfusion of five units of blood, she was able to undergo emergency surgery and start the slow process of recovery.

But those challenges paled next to the hardest thing she and her husband faced: over a period of months, a few members in the new church where her husband pastored had secretively gathered a handful of people around them to plan a public rejection of his leadership. In twenty-five years of ministry, her husband had been appreciated and respected. Now they were experiencing a painful betrayal by the very people they'd come to serve.

As Sue's health was returning, the unity within the church was disintegrating. All the while, the stress on her husband was growing. Finally he collapsed one windy, winter morning at the side of a road where he'd stopped to help a motorist with a stalled car. Later that day at the hospital, tests revealed he was very ill with diabetes. Feeling alone and overwhelmed, they decided he should resign his pastorate, a decision that left him sick and jobless. But after a number of months, Sue unpacked the moving boxes in a different home, and her husband started a new job in a place where the aching pain in her heart was the only thing that wasn't new. She wondered if it would ever go away.

She pulled a stack of books out of a box, and her prayer journal from several months earlier fell out. As she read, the healing began to unfold. She read what she had written on all the days when she had poured out her heart to the Lord. She read about the times when she'd felt led to drive to the streets where those who attacked her and her husband lived. She had parked a few houses down, remaining in her car, and had prayed and prayed and prayed for the people who'd hurt them. Daily, on her knees, she'd written her prayers and the burdens and desires of her heart.

Now she could close her journal—knowing she'd done all she could do. In that moment, she offered God a prayer of thankfulness. For whatever reason, she thanked him for allowing her to share in his suffering and thanked him that their tumultuous year came when the focus of her life was to spend time with him in prayer. When she had made that her goal she couldn't have known that a lot of the year would be spent praying for her enemies. But God had carried her through with his love, provision, companionship, and direction, even in their suffering, and had brought them into a new season with fresh possibilities, renewed hope, and open doors that they would have never dreamed of.[4]

When we obey Christ's command to pray for our enemies and to forgive them, we not only receive rewards in heaven but also blessings in this life: We'll be freer emotionally, healthier physically, and more able to experience the joy of Jesus. We'll be drawn closer to him, see him work in amazing ways, and experience the power of forgiveness in our own life.

QUESTIONS FOR DISCUSSION OR JOURNALING

1. When we pray for those who hurt us, God performs a miracle in our heart, replacing anger and resentment with his grace and freedom. When have you prayed for an "enemy," and what did God do?

2. As you read the stories in this chapter, did they remind you of a

person who hurt or betrayed you whom you could begin to pray for right now? Add his or her name to your VIP prayer list and purpose to forgive him or her. What is a verse you could pray when this person comes to mind? It's never too late to begin. Be sure to share or write the results of your journey.

3. When you think about Jesus's telling us to forgive our enemies and pray for them, how do you feel: encouraged, anxious, mad, indifferent, or some other emotion? What do you sense he would want you to do with your response?

4. Look up and read: Matthew 6:12–15; Mark 11:24–25; Ephesians 4:32; 1 John 1:6–9, 2:5–6, 9–11. What do these verses tell you?

12

Living in Continual Prayer

Paul does not ask us to spend some of every day in prayer. No, Paul is much more radical. He asks us to pray day and night, in joy and in sorrow, at work and at play, without intermissions or breaks. For Paul, prayer is like breathing.

—Henri Nouwen

Pam was scheduled to teach a Bible Study at 10:00 a.m., and she didn't feel at all prepared. She needed more time to review the lesson and get everything organized so the class would go smoothly. As she pored over her notes again, a feeling of urgency suddenly swept over her. She knew instantly that she must get to the Children's Center, the pediatric nursing center where her multihandicapped daughter, Jan, lived. Jan's daily care was critical, as was that of all the children at this long-term nursing center. So, thinking God was prompting her to go because Jan was sick, Pam gathered her things and left, praying as she drove the five miles through the congested morning traffic. She thought about her daughter, but she also wondered, *Who needs my prayers today?*

Arriving at the center, Pam found her daughter in her bed sleeping peacefully with no hint of a problem. In fact, Jan was better than she had been the whole month, the nurse told her. *I really misunderstood you this time, Lord,* Pam thought. Feeling confused by the strong urging she'd experienced to go there, Pam slid into the chair beside Jan's bed.

After a few minutes she looked across the room at one of Jan's roommates. The little girl's daddy was standing over her hospital bed, stroking her face. From her labored breathing and swollen body, Pam realized she was dying. She soon learned that the girl's daddy had flown in from California to be with her.

Pam's heart broke as she saw this tall, tough biker kind of guy with tattoos covering both arms standing there all alone, tears streaking down his face. She walked over and began to talk to the dad. Pam told him how much she and her husband loved his little girl and what a blessing it had been to sing "Twinkle, Twinkle Little Star" to her over the past months and watch for the twinkle that song always brought to her eyes.

The dad, Larry, then began to talk to Pam as if he knew her. One of the things he said was, "I've almost learned the words to 'Jesus Loves Me' from your daughter's cassette tape."

Slowly the situation came into focus for Pam.

Jan had lived at home for almost seventeen years, and when she moved into the Children's Center, Pam and her husband, Mike, had wanted their voices to comfort Jan in their absence. They'd recorded all her favorite songs, and "Jesus Loves Me" was on the tape at least five different places because Jan loved to hear it so much. That tape played twenty-four hours a day in her room, complete with their son's voice, the dog barking, and other background sounds from their home. *Poor Larry has been a captive audience to our off-key singing now for many hours; that's why he feels he knows me,* Pam thought.

Quietly she asked Larry if she could pray with him, not knowing that the staff had already attempted to talk to him about spiritual things and he'd rejected their efforts every time.

"It don't matter," he answered, as she began praying. Later he accepted a booklet of comforting scriptures she had written in calligraphy.

As Pam drove off to her Bible study, she contemplated the nudging she'd felt earlier. Because of her simple prayer of compassion, a man's life was touched in one of the most desperate moments of his life. From heaven's perspective, her meeting with Larry was probably a lot more fruitful than an extra hour of preparation for her Bible class that day.

Pam didn't consider herself to have "arrived" in her prayer life, but she had learned that she could talk and listen to God anywhere, at any time: when she was studying or cooking, while she watched her son play baseball from the stands, as she was driving, or during her visits with Jan at the nursing center. This kind of unbroken communion with the Lord doesn't happen overnight but develops day by day, step by step in our spiritual journey. We draw near to the Lord, and he draws near to us, as he's promised (see James 4:8 NASB). We sense his presence guiding us through our day, and respond to his loving nudges. And he always does more than we could ask or imagine, according to his riches in glory in Christ Jesus (see Ephesians 3:20–21).

PRACTICING GOD'S PRESENCE

Brother Lawrence, a humble, seventeenth-century monk known best for his little book *The Practice of the Presence of God,* worked in the kitchen of a monastery, where he discovered the secret of how we can live joyfully with God while on the earth. He believed prayer was simply having a continuing sense of God's presence and talking with him throughout the day, and that's what Brother Lawrence did while he cooked the meals and served the food.

Brother Lawrence wrote, "We should offer our work to Him before we begin and thank Him afterward for the privilege of having done it for His sake. The continuous conversation should also include praising and loving God incessantly for His infinite goodness and protection."[1] He believed it was a big mistake to think of prayer time as being different (or better or worse) when it occurred in the midst of our activities instead of in quiet devotions. His view of prayer reminds me of the comparison some books on sleep systems make between the sleep a baby gets in her car seat while you're driving and her sleep in the crib.

"I was told that any sleep my infant gets that's not in her crib is 'junk sleep,'" a young mother told me.

I don't know what a baby might think of that logic, but some of the most rested little ones I've seen have awakened from a nice nap in their mother's arms, a gentle bouncy chair, or a car seat. Similarly, I don't think Brother Lawrence would say that all our prayers said outside of our prayer chair are "junk prayers."

On the contrary, those prayers can be very effective.

PRAYING ANYWHERE

Paul said, "In every place men [and women] should pray" (1 Timothy 2:8 AMP), and, "Pray all the time; thank God no matter what happens" (1 Thessalonians 5:17–18 MSG). He didn't confine praying to just the intercessors' room or the prayer chapel. He said you can spread prayer to every part of your life. Your computer desk can become a prayer nook. The dining table can become a family altar as you talk to God together about the challenges you're each facing at work or school. Your kitchen can be a holy place where you commune with God and bless the food as it is prepared.

On your commute to work, you can make space for the Lord, requesting his guidance for your day and later, down the road, for his mercy for the injured when you hear a siren. On the way home, when you pass an empty lot, let it remind you to roll your burdens onto him so you don't walk in the door and dump your work-related stress on your family members.

Right where you are at this moment is a great place to pray.

Janis is one of the busiest women I know. Besides her own eight children, she takes in foster infants awaiting adoption. As we began to talk one day, I wondered how she prayed at all, much less prayed "without ceasing," as the King James Version translates Paul's instruction in 1 Thessalonians 5:17. For Janis, it means to *always* be prayerful. For example, talking to the Lord works well when she's up for early morning infant feedings, because everyone else in the household is asleep at that hour. But that's only one part of her prayer regimen. Her motto is, Whatever situation arises, *pray*!

When a person comes to her mind, she prays for him or her. Her day is peppered with quick "dart prayers" such as, "Lord, help me respond to this child in a way that pleases you. Let me be your hands and feet," and, "Lord, I forgive this person right now, this instant. Please forgive my critical spirit, and fill me with your love." These dart prayers find their way to God's ear just as our longer, more comprehensive prayers do.

The important thing about prayer, says Richard Foster, is "to believe that God can reach us and bless us in the ordinary junctures of daily life. . . . You see, the only place God can bless us is *right where we are*." He urges us to "carry on an ongoing conversation with God about the daily stuff of life."[2] We all need times alone with God, but when long periods of solitude aren't possible, put all your energy into even the brief moments.[3] Talk to God about the challenges you face, the details of your day. (He cares about the little things as well as the big stuff.) Give him your hurts and disappointments; share your thankfulness for blessings and beautiful things you see along the way. That's living in continual prayer.

Praying through Your Busy Day

Here are some ways you can practice God's presence and carry on an ongoing conversation with him no matter where you are.

Let Your Daily Tasks Draw You to Prayer

While she washes the dishes, Caroline thanks God for the gift of salvation and that Christ is continually cleansing her from sin.

Although they live in different parts of the country, two close friends pray for each other every morning as they make their beds. They were heartbroken when one of them had to move to another state. There would be no more picnic lunches in the park with their kids, no more girls' nights out at Starbucks, no more meeting at each other's home to pray together for their concerns and blessings.

But as the friends dried their tears and talked about the change that lay ahead, they realized prayer could keep them heart to heart, even across the miles. They decided to pray for each other as they made their beds each morning, and they would also exchange lots of e-mails to see how God was working in each other's life. Although they've lived far apart now for several years, they've never lost the closeness that comes from caring and praying for each other's needs.

Ask God for grace to do your duties with a good attitude, and "work heartily," as if you're working for the Lord (Ephesians 6:5–7 MSG). Commit that very work to him and ask for his blessing on it.

Look for Prayer Cues

You may not have a child in any of the schools you pass by, but somebody's kids go there, and they all need prayer. Teachers desperately need wisdom today to deal with the many problems they face. (For the first time in history, teachers now can get homicide insurance—and they need prayers for protection, as do the students.) Pray also for the school's principal and staff. Ask God to bring every person in that school out of darkness and into his light. You have to slow down anyway, so when you see a school-zone sign, think *prayer zone*, and put some energy into those brief moments of caring as you drive through it.

My prayer partner Peggy uses all sorts of cues to remind her to pray. When she puts on her seat belt before heading to the high school to substitute teach, she says, "Lord, I want to abide in you and be yoked with you." When she stops at a stop sign, she takes a deep breath and prays, "My rest is in you alone, Lord. I may be trying to get somewhere, but thank you for preparing the way." When she pulls weeds in her garden, she says, "Lord, keep the cares of this life from choking out your Word and rendering my life unfruitful. Help our family grow according to your plan for us."

When my friend Janet goes to the beauty shop for a haircut, she prays for those who've lost their hair because of cancer and thanks God for the health and stamina he has given her.

When I suggested to a woman in Massachusetts that she could let the shower be her cue as she begins her day, she adapted Psalm 51:9–11 (KJV) as her prayer the very next morning: "Lord, create in me a clean heart and renew a right spirit within me; cleanse me of sin." As she prayed in the shower, all of a sudden a number of sins flooded her mind, and one by one, she confessed each one to God. She began to weep and gave him her shame for past misdeeds and failures; she named the people she'd been angry at, and asked God to forgive her for harboring resentment.

When she stepped out of the shower that day, she was truly clean—a new person in Christ Jesus. The old had passed away, and the new had come (see 2 Corinthians 5:17). Her friend had been dragging her to church every Sunday for quite a while, but she hadn't experienced any sense of connection with Jesus. All that changed when she used the simple means of her daily shower and a passage of Scripture to connect with God in prayer.

Prayer Drive

Kenda prays for loved ones as she sees the same model and color as the vehicle they drive. When she sees a vintage Cutlass like her husband drives, it reminds her to thank God for him and to pray for his workday. When she sees a Yukon, she prays for her parents. Red Suburbans are cues to pray for her sister and her family. And a green Dodge Ram truck reminds her to pray for her pastor. She also pays attention to billboards and radio commercials to refocus her heart toward circumstances she needs to pray about. This woman does a lot of praying while she's just doing errands around town.

When Kenda passes wooden fences, it reminds her that Christians are held together by the Holy Spirit and by the sacrifice Jesus made for us, and she asks God to make repairs and improvements as needed in the body of Christ. "Whenever I see a fence being built or repaired I remember that Jesus is very handy with nails and wood and that he specializes in restoring people and churches," Kenda says.

Develop a Heart for Your Neighbors

When Margaret moved into her new neighborhood seven years ago, she didn't know a single person on the block. A friend suggested that, when she walked, she be intentional about praying for her neighbors. As a result, in the last seven years, Margaret has prayed scores of prayers for those who live around her: for the man on the corner who is all alone, for the woman across the street whose husband died unexpectedly last November, for the teenager next door who seems to be in the rough waters of adolescence.

She has found that praying for those around her has given her a real heart for her neighbors, and they have opened their hearts to her in a way she never expected. "It's hard *not* to care about your neighbors if you're praying for them," she told me.

Pray through the News

When you're reading the newspaper or watching the news, ask God to highlight something you need to be praying about for your city, your nation, or a hot spot in the world. Cut out the headline and stick it in your Bible. Let it remind you to ask God's mercy and help for a wounded soldier, a school embroiled in problems, a family that lost its home in a fire, or for any other need depicted in the news story. If you're watching a local news broadcast and see a victim of a crime or tragedy, mute the TV and pray on the spot for that person, or wait for a commercial break. It's amazing how your prayers can impact the world just from where you sit in your living room.

Make Your Work Space a Prayer Bench

Roberta is a sales rep who is on the road many days a month selling wholesale travel packages to corporations and businesses. No matter where she is, when she turns on her computer, a window opens with a daily devotional reading, and she has set the screensaver to feature a favorite Scripture verse. She also keeps a few Bible verses on her desktop that shape her prayers during the day. As the computer boots up—and before she plows into her stacks of invoices or her must-do list—she takes a few moments to ask God to guide her and give her wisdom for the different situations with clients she'll have that day. Those moments make all the difference in centering her on what really matters.

Make a Mobile Quiet-Time Basket

Sometimes we say we can't have time with God because our kids are around. Alisha had three children close together and little time alone by herself—plus she was homeschooling. So after breakfast each day and before school time, she'd get out her mobile quiet-time basket, which held her Bible and her prayer journal plus pens and paper, and would go wherever the children wanted to play—in the playroom, outside on sunny days, or in the family room.

While they played, Alisha read her Bible, prayed, and wrote a verse or thought in her journal. Not only did this routine put Alisha in a calmer state of mind, but she was also providing a wonderful role model to her children. (Since prayer is *caught* more than *taught*, your activities as a role model are the number-one most powerful things you can do to teach your children that talking to God is an important part of your day.) During homeschool, Alisha and the children committed their lessons and assignments to God. Later they prayed together about math problems the kids were stuck on and asked for help when it was needed or when tempers flared.

Many children don't ever see their parents spending time with God because it's usually easier to do when the children are asleep or the parent is alone. But Alisha's children, now teenagers with the oldest in college, grew up seeing their mother communicate easily and often with the One who created them. If they saw that she was having a hard day, they would ask if they could pray for her. And along the way, they were learning how to spend time with God themselves in the midst of their busy schedules and also developing a lifelong habit of prayer.

Praying throughout your day will bring great benefits. It will help you remember that God is present with you wherever you are, that he is working in your life and in the lives of people around you. Regardless of when and how God works, whether he answers your prayers in the way you want him to or you have to wait a long time for the answer, whether you experience an unsettling turn of events or jump for joy when your heart's desire is fulfilled, you have much to thank God for. We all do. So don't forget to thank him for his goodness and faithfulness.

My Prayer for You

The praying life isn't a life cloistered away from the sounds of the world. Prayer is the language of the heart in communion with God throughout our busy days—in the midst of the noise and the bustle of people and the places we go and into the evening hours. "To pray is nothing more involved than to let Jesus come into our hearts, to give him access with all his power to our needs," said O. Hallesby.[4] Prayer, he said, should be the means by which we receive all that we need, and for this reason, it can be our daily refuge and daily consolation, our daily joy and source of rich and inexhaustible joy in life.[5]

In this book we've discussed how prayer is not another duty to perform or a burden we're saddled with in an already packed schedule. Prayer is a priceless gift, and it's all about relationship. It's the Lord's incredible invitation to let him carry our burdens and worries. Besides all that, prayer releases God's power and brings his grace and help to us in our earthly needs and the needs of others.

What a privilege we have to go to the Lord in prayer and ask him to not only show his mighty power in the world but to change our own hearts so we become more like Jesus! And perhaps best of all, prayer's effects will last long after we have ended our journey on earth. Our prayers will go on blessing countless people we've loved and prayed for; these prayers will outlive our lives and our world. And with every prayer, we will get to know, love, and enjoy God more and more—and receive his unfailing love for us more fully.

Here's my prayer for you as we end this book:

May the God of our Lord Jesus Christ, the glorious Father, give you the Spirit of wisdom and revelation so that you may know him better. I pray that the eyes of your heart may be enlightened so you may know the hope to which he has called you, the riches of his glorious inheritance in the saints, and his incomparably great power for those who believe [see Ephesians 1:17–19]. *And in all the days ahead, may the God of hope fill you with all joy and peace as you trust in him so that you may overflow with hope by the power of the Holy Spirit* [see Romans 15:13]. *Amen.*

Questions for Discussion and Journaling

1. What are the most helpful concepts you've learned in *A Busy Woman's Guide to Prayer?*

2. How has discovering or applying this truth impacted or changed your life?

3. Using one of the ideas from this chapter, how can you put into practice Paul's admonition to "pray without ceasing" this week?

4. How could your life with God as a family reflect or apply something you have discovered about prayer?

5. What have you learned about the practice of prayer that you could pass on to someone younger in age or younger in his or her faith?

Notes

1. A Mary Heart with a Martha Schedule

1. Adapted from "Make Your Home a Power House" in *H.O.P.E. 5X5X5 Plan*, a booklet published by the Lighthouse Movement. Call 800-217-5200 to order.

2. The Gift of Prayer

1. "Families struggle to find time for little moments," *Cincinnati Enquirer,* Sunday, March 20, 2005, A14

2. Martin Smith, "God Is a Conversation," *Union Life* magazine, May/June, 1993, 8.

3. Sam Storms, "God's Greatest Joy," *Pray!* magazine, May/June 2005, 8.

4. Oswald Chambers, *My Utmost for His Highest* (Westwood, NJ: Barbour, 1963), 241.

5. Dutch Sheets, *The Beginner's Guide to Intercession* (Ann Arbor, MI: Servant, 2001), 11.

6. Rosalind Rinker, *Prayer: Conversing with God* (Grand Rapids, MI: Zondervan, 1959), 23.

7. Alice Smith, *Beyond the Veil* (Ventura, CA: Renew Books/Gospel Light, 1997), 74–75.

8. Anne Graham Lotz, "My Heart's Cry," *Fresh Outlook* magazine, November/December 2003, 46.

9. Storms, "God's Greatest Joy," 8.

10. Jean E. Syswerda, gen. ed., *The Prayer Bible* (Wheaton, IL: Tyndale, 2003), 1,427.

3. The Invitation of Prayer

1. Kay Peters, *The Wonder of It All* (Oklahoma City: self-published, 1980), 123. Used by permission of Patty J. Johnston.

2. Ibid., 123–24.

notes

3. Luci Swindoll, quoted in the Women of Faith Study Guide *Living Above Worry and Stress* (Nashville: Thomas Nelson, 2003), 10.

4. Corrie ten Boom, *Reflections of God's Glory* (Grand Rapids, MI: Zondervan, 1999), 37.

5. John Piper, *Pierced by the Word* (Sisters, OR: Multnomah, 2003), 47.

6. Ibid., 49–50.

7. Henri J. M. Nouwen, *The Only Necessary Thing: Living a Prayerful Life,* comp. and ed. Wendy Wilson Greer (New York: Crossroad, 1999), 165.

8. Lynne Hammond and Patsy Camenti, *Secrets to Powerful Prayer* (Tulsa: Harrison House, 2000), 25.

9. Edith Schaeffer, "The Meaning of Meditation," in *One Holy Passion,* ed. Judith Couchman (Colorado Springs: Waterbrook, 1998), 61.

4. The Power of Prayer

1. Jack R. Taylor, *Much More* (Nashville: Broadman, 1972), 79.

2. Ibid., 81.

3. Derek Prince, *Derek Prince on Experiencing God's Power* (New Kensington, PA: Whitaker House, 1998), 374–77.

4. Source unknown.

5. O. Hallesby, *Prayer* (Minneapolis: Augsburg Fortress, 1994), 153, 13.

6. Del Fehsenfeld, "Unleashing the Power of Prayer," *Pray!* magazine, July/August 2004, 47.

5. The Longevity of Prayer

1. Hallesby, *Prayer,* 172–73.

2. E. M. Bounds, *The Possibilities of Prayer* (Springdale, PA: Whitaker House, 1994).

3. Wesley Duewel, *Mighty Prevailing Prayer* (Grand Rapids, MI: Zondervan, 1990), 151–52.

4. Alice and Eddie Smith, *Drawing Closer to God's Heart* (Lake Mary, FL: Strang, 2002), 89.

5. Edward K. Rowell, *Fresh Illustrations for Preaching and Teaching* (Grand Rapids, MI: Baker, 1997), 165.

6. E. M. Bounds, quoted in *The Praying Heart: Thoughts on Prayer to Draw the Heart of God* (Bloomington, MN: Garborg's Heart 'n' Home, 1989), September 1.

notes

7. Dick Eastman, *Love on Its Knees* (Tarrytown, NY: Chosen, 1989), 18.
8. Ibid.
9. Hallesby, quoted in *The Praying Heart*, June 17.

6. Praying with a Godward Focus

1. With grateful acknowledgment to our son, Navy Lt. Christopher Fuller, for sharing his personal essay, "War and Medicine," which gave me a vivid glimpse of the realities of combat and provided details included in this part of the story.
2. Martha Thatcher, "Getting God into Focus," in *One Holy Passion*, 142.
3. Corrie ten Boom, *Reflections of God's Glory*, 92.
4. Chambers, *My Utmost for His Highest*, 157.
5. Go to www.momsintouch.org if you would like information on Moms In Touch International groups in your community or on how to start a MITI group.
6. Judson Cornwall, *Praying the Scriptures* (Lake Mary, FL: Creation House, 1988), 84.
7. M. Basilea Schlink, *Praying Our Way through Life* (Darmstadt-Eberstadt, Germany: Evangelical Sisterhood of Mary, 1991), 9.
8. Charles Spurgeon, quoted in *Prayer Portions for Daily Living*, ed. Charles Cook (Chicago: Moody Press, 1978), 33.
9. For further study, see the excellent resource "Names of God: 21 Names of God and Their Meanings," a 2003 pamphlet available from Rose Publishing, Torrence, California; www.rose-publishing.com.

7. Connecting with God in a Noisy, Fast-Paced World

1. Brent W. Bost, MD, *The Hurried Woman Syndrome* (New York: McGraw Hill, 2005), 3–5.
2. My paraphrase of Luke 10:41–42.
3. Andrew Murray, *With Christ in the School of Prayer* (Springdale, PA: Whitaker House, 1981), 172.
4. Corrie ten Boom, *Reflections of God's Glory*, 79.
5. Adapted from Catherine Marshall, *Something More* (New York: Guideposts, 1974), 83–89.

notes

6. Margaret Therkelsen, *Realizing the Presence of the Spirit* (Grand Rapids, MI: Revell, 1998), 120–21.

7. "Lois Prater's Childhood Missionary Dream Is Fulfilled—at Age 76," *Charisma* magazine, May 2002, 19–20.

8. Getting Out of the Box: Finding Your Spiritual Pathway

1. Bill Hybels, *Too Busy Not to Pray* (Downers Grove, IL: InterVarsity Press, 1988), 104.

2. Andrew Murray, *The Inner Life* (Springdale, PA: Whitaker House, 1984), 21.

3. To order this bandana for your deployed loved one, visit www.psalm91bandana.com.

4. Chambers, *My Utmost for His Highest*, 133.

5. Dean Merrill, "Whatever Happened to Kneeling?" *Pray!* magazine, May/June 2005, 35.

6. Prince, *Derek Prince on Experiencing God's Power*, 299–328.

7. Jim Cymbala and Dean Merrill, *Fresh Power* (Grand Rapids, MI: Zondervan, 2001), 78.

9. P-U-S-H! Praying the Distance

1. Murray, *With Christ in the School of Prayer*, 119.

2. Duewel, *Mighty Prevailing Prayer*, 152.

3. Murray, *With Christ in the School of Prayer*, 119.

4. Joseph Parker, quoted in *Prayer Portions*, 110.

5. Duewel, *Mighty Prevailing Prayer*, 158.

6. Murray, *With Christ in the School of Prayer*, 121.

7. My thanks to Martha Singleton for sharing this true story with me.

8. Adapted from Cheri Fuller, "Praying the Distance," in *PrayKids* (issue on perseverance), March 2005, 1–2.

10. Praying on the Spot

1. Chambers, *My Utmost for His Highest*, 178.

2. Joe Martin, "Unbroken Communion with God," *Pray!* magazine, September/October 2004, 31.

3. Amy Carmichael, *Gold by Moonlight* (Fort Washington, PA: Christian Literature Crusade, 1935), quoted in *One Holy Passion*, comp. Judith Couchman (Colorado Springs: Waterbrook, 1998), 205.

11. Praying for Your Enemies: The Clean-Slate Principle
  1. Corrie ten Boom, *Reflections of God's Glory,* 27–28.
  2. D. L. Moody, quoted in Neva Coyle, "The Power of Confession," in *One Holy Passion*, 88–89.
  3. Cindy Jacobs, "The Clean-Heart Principle," in *One Holy Passion,* 94.
  4. My thanks to "Sue" for allowing me to include her experience in this book. If you would like to know more about her story, visit www.womanofjoy.com.

12. Living in Continual Prayer
  1. Brother Lawrence, *The Practice of the Presence of God* (New Kensington, PA: Whitaker House, 1982), 25.
  2. Richard Foster, *Prayer: Finding the Heart's True Home* (New York: HarperCollins, 1992), 11.
  3. Ibid., 12.
  4. Hallesby, *Prayer,* 152.
  5. Ibid., 38.

About the Author

CHERI FULLER is a popular speaker and award-winning author of more than thirty books including *A Fresh Vision of Jesus, The One-Year Book of Praying Through the Bible, Fearless: Building a Faith that Overcomes Your Fear, When Mothers Pray,* and The School Saavy Kids series. Fuller is a prolific author who also has written hundreds of articles for magazines such as *Family Circle, Focus on the Family, Pray!, Guideposts, Moody, ParentLife,* and other publications. She has been a frequent guest on national radio and TV programs including *Focus on the Family, At Home-Live! Family Life Today, 700 Club, Moody Midday Connection,* and many others.

Cheri's ministry, Families Pray USA, inspires and equips people of all ages to impact their world through prayer. She reaches out to hundreds of audiences through her dynamic combination of biblical wisdom, humor, storytelling, and creative ideas for real life. She is a contributing writer for *Today's Christian Woman,* and her Web site, www.CheriFuller.com, features her monthly column, "Mothering by Heart," as well as a free Bible study on prayer and other resources on prayer and inspiration.

about the author

She and her husband, Holmes, live in Oklahoma, where Cheri was honored as Oklahoma Mother of the Year in 2004.

To schedule Cheri for speaking engagements or conferences, contact Speak Up Speaker Services at 810-982-0898 or e-mail speakupinc@aol.com.